Wising Up:

The Mistakes Women Make in Business and How to Avoid Them

Also by Jo Foxworth

BOSS LADY: AN EXECUTIVE WOMAN
TALKS ABOUT MAKING IT

Wising Up:

The Mistakes Women Make in Business and How to Avoid Them

Jo Foxworth

Illustrations by Marvin Glass

Delacorte Press/New York

Published by
Delacorte Press
1 Dag Hammarskjold Plaza
New York, N.Y. 10017

Manufactured in the United States of America

First printing

Designed by Laura Bernay

Library of Congress Cataloging in Publication Data

Foxworth, Jo.
  Wising up.

  Includes index.
  1. Women in business—United States.
2. Women executives—United States. 3. Success.
I. Title.
HF5500.3.U54F69   650.1′4′088042   80–17864
ISBN 0–440–09605–7

This book is dedicated to two women of tomorrow with the hope that they will know what they want and go for it in the world they inherit. They are Kim Mitchell of Fort Worth and Kana Fukuhara of Tokyo.

Acknowledgment

Any author is expected, out of courtesy and decency, to acknowledge all assistance with a manuscript and thank the people who gave it. There is nothing courteous or decent about this acknowledgment, just the bald admission that I could not have written a book or anything else without the continuing help of Eileen Harrold and Neb Suito. I am grateful to them beyond expression and, although I am sure they know it already, I take particular pleasure in saying so publicly.

Contents

Introduction

It doesn't make sense. We live in a society whose traditions cause us to go on killing one whole sex with overwork and, at the same time, boring the other sex half to death with underuse. I am made depressingly aware of this every day, never more forcibly than on a recent evening in St. Louis where I was attending a conference of the American Advertising Federation.

The conference was in the old Chase Plaza, a hotel distinguished principally by its history and size. It is big enough to accommodate several conventions at a time, and among those holding forth that weekend was something I had never heard of before: a convention of grandmothers.

The suite I was sharing with Irma Strzelec and Patricia Mansfield had a door with a soul of its own. It could be opened by only one of the three keys we had been provided and that one had to be "kitzled" in the lock while somebody delivered a series of sharp kicks to a particular point near the bottom of the door.

I approached it early one evening while wearing open-toed shoes and was standing there wondering if it was worth a broken toe to get in, when along came a white-haired woman in jeans, Western shirt, and cowboy boots.

"What's the matter, kid?" she asked. "Locked out?"

I sheepishly explained my plight, whereupon she delivered one swift, authoritative kick to the offending door and it promptly flew open. In gratitude I invited her in for a drink, and over a glass of bourbon she told me about the grandmothers' convention.

Some of her story you know already. There are literally thousands of grandmothers roaming the earth on life insurance money, hunting somebody to talk to and something to do. Naturally, they've inherited problems along with the insurance money, and these St. Louis conventioneers had banded together in an association with officers, committees, and a program to provide mutual help in finding some solutions. No storybook grannies were there. They were much too full of moxie to become a drag on their families or wait around for a terminal illness. They were doing something about a situation that's getting bigger than all of us.

I've thought about that convention a lot. There are so many grandmothers in the country that a national association of them is in order. *Question: Where are the grandfathers?*

If the answer to that one can't change some of our idiot-thinking about women in business, "Cheers, Grandmother!" And, "Grand-dad, R.I.P."

You've Got to Know the Territory

"What am I doing wrong?"

All over the country the question echoes—a poignant plaint, a bewildered protest, an astonished demand. You hear it every day from frustrated career women who moved confidently into jobs that appeared promising but turned out to be big, flat disappointments.

Frances flung herself into a chair beside me at one of those numberless women's business seminars and spelled it out. We were in Chicago, but I've heard the same basic story from Boston to Seattle, in big cities and small ones. "Look at me," Frances said. "I'm twenty-eight years old. I'm attractive enough and smart enough and I've got an MBA. Everybody said you need an MBA, so okay, I went back to school and got it. Right away I landed what looked like a good job with a famous company. I felt lucky because the recruiter said

I had an exciting future there and I couldn't see any reason why not. But after three years—*three years!*— I'm in the same old pigeonhole, doing the same old things and bored out of my mind. I've had two piddling raises but I still can't afford an apartment of my own— a place that's just mine—and I have to share with these two roommates who drive me up the wall. I've got to get out of this rut I'm in—but how? Two men my age who started out with the company at the same time I did have gone up like rockets! Tell me—what am I doing wrong?"

Listen, Frances, I hate to say this, but why pretend? As matters stand now, the business world is male ter- ritory. The men call the shots. Right or wrong, it's *their turf* and you don't need a sociologist, anthropologist, or any other kind of ologist to brief you on male territorial rights. The competition for control of any given area can be, and usually is, fierce—in the jungle or in the most "civilized" citadels of commerce.

Women stepping onto this alien turf for the first time may suddenly find themselves up to the armpits in quicksand. This comes as a swift and distinct shock to many an ambitious woman who has overestimated the gender breakthrough and confidently expected to land in the fast lane, leading straight to the seats of heavy money and strong professional punch. The last thing she expected was quicksand.

It is no disgrace to have overestimated the gender breakthrough. Women have become a genuine media event. Particularly career women, who have been hymned by the print and broadcast press as the New Achievers. Newspapers, magazines, radio programs, and television shows, all hungry for provocative material and quick to respond to each other's subject matter, have made so much of the women's movement (with emphasis on the occasional female "success" in business) that it is easy enough to assume that women *have it made*.

Don't you believe it. Nobody has anything made in the business world, even the highest-ranking men. It can all come unmade overnight, like the very bed you sleep in. Companies are sold. Mergers occur. Somebody retires, dies, commits suicide, absconds with the funds, or cracks up on learning that his only begotten son is a junkie. Any of these things can send shock waves through an organization, changing the power structure completely. There are "Watergates" of one kind and another all through business—seemingly obscure incidents that destroy the existing order, causing some stars to set and others to rise dramatically. The trouble with being on top of the world is that the world does turn and staying there takes some scrambling.

Elementary as all this is, most women don't realize it. Men do, because it's their turf and they know their way around on it. This is another reason why they are antsy about their territorial rights in business and why they do not welcome competition of any kind from either sex. If they are especially resentful of competition imposed by law or industry ruling, it is probably because they feel that the odds are being spread against them by forces beyond their control.

The very clichés of the territory are misleading. Perhaps the most confused and confusing of the lot is the one we hear most often: "Business is business!" It is pronounced with such ringing conviction and finality that it is almost always accepted as definitive, the inarguable conclusion to any disagreement or discussion.

"Business is business!" is not a definition at all. It is an excuse, usually offered for an action or inaction the person on the receiving end probably isn't going to like at all. It's why somebody has to work tonight or Sunday, why a raise isn't coming through after all, why a social obligation is chickened out on, or why some other promise isn't going to be kept. When you get the word, you may not like it, but the declaration implies that nothing can be done about it. What it really means is that nothing is going to be done about it and there's nothing you can do about that, either! It's like the current rhetorical query: "What can I tell you?" or "What are you gonna do?"

One young woman told me it was what the personnel director said to her when she was dismissed from her job as assistant product manager at a food company in Minneapolis. "Sales are off—and you know how it is. Business is business!" A friend of hers at the company reported that a new man came in to take her job the week after she left. He was a relative of one of the company vice-presidents. So much for what business is!

Actually, business isn't even businesslike, in spite of all the systems, forms, memos, contracts, and ritualized meetings. If it were businesslike, there wouldn't be nearly so many broken promises making it necessary to haul out the old shopworn but inarguable excuse.

The truth is that most companies operate in a state of continuing confusion—some caused by carelessness

and garden-variety inefficiency, some deliberately created by people whose secret motto is "Confuse and
Conquer." Not only is there a "hidden agenda" at most
meetings, there are usually unstated objectives and
unrevealed corporate plans. If this sounds like the place
where you work, be advised that it is not unique. Behind the facade of orderliness and civility at almost any
company in the country, the activity is usually as fre-
netic as the panicky scurrying you encounter when you
turn over a rock in the woods. It's why the most frequently seen office sign in America reads: "You Don't
Have to Be Crazy to Work Here—But It Helps!" Yet I
know women whose low opinion of their own capability is reinforced by the shambles at the companies
where they are employed. They actually feel that no
"sane" company will tolerate them!

Simply put, *business is trade*. It is a simple matter of
trading something you have for something you want
more. Time and skills are exchanged for money, money
for goods and services, goods and services for money—
and money for time and skills. The exchanges, ostensi-
bly, are for the mutual benefit of the exchangers, and
companies are organized to conduct them for the
convenience of all concerned. But in the business world
there are few equal swaps. Usually it is the best trader
who wins—and the sex of the winner is almost never
female.

The inequities in the exchanges are nowhere more
glaringly evident than in the differences between the
genders in status and pay. Twenty years into the
strongest Women's Revolution in history, the progress
of women in business is a mere drop in the proverbial

bucket. Yes, half of the great American work force now *is* female. Yes, there *are* women in the ranks of the military; also at West Point, Annapolis, and NASA— put there forcibly by law and, for the most part, openly resented (at West Point and other areas of the military to the extent of sexist hazing). Yes, there *are* hundreds of women in jobs that nobody would have dreamed of giving them ten years ago and a great many of them are doing this "man's work" better than the men who pre- ceded them.

In the New York radio market, for instance, five years ago you could hardly find a female sales representative. Now almost all the reps are women. A top executive at one of the stations told me this is because management is convinced that the women work harder, keep better records, take shorter lunch hours, turn in less boggling expense accounts, and sell at least as many, often more, commercials. It should be observed, however, that in the television industry, where the pickings are better for sales people, the rep staffs are still almost 100 per- cent male. Does this mean that men who sell television time have work habits more endearing to management? Or that the male time salesmen are more resistant to the female invasion in areas where the rewards are richer?

Although women have been, and are, demonstrating their effectiveness virtually everywhere, the facts are, balefully, these:

According to the United States Department of Labor, women earn only fifty-nine cents for every dol- lar earned by men. In technical and professional jobs median weekly income of women working full time in

1979 was 73 percent that of men and in sales jobs, 45 percent. Women college graduates had a median income of $10,861 while their male counterparts got $17,891. Among executives paid $25,000 and up per year, only 2.3 percent were women, and among managers, 5 percent.

True, women did achieve some noteworthy "firsts" in the seventies and the press gasped out the news in a lather of excitement worthy of the fact that these things had happened for the very first time: Chicago got a woman mayor, Jane M. Byrne; Colorado, a woman Supreme Court Justice, Jean Eberhart Dubofsky; the Milwaukee Press Club, a woman president, Beth Slocum; Sigma Delta Chi, the Society of Professional Journalists (which admitted women only a decade ago), a woman president, Jean Otto; the University of Missouri, a woman chancellor, Dr. Barbara Uehling; the American Academy and Institute of Art and Letters, a woman president, author-historian Barbara Tuchman; and the Jewish faith, a woman rabbi, Linda Joy Holzman, who also became the first woman in the nation to be presiding rabbi of a temple. Everybody seemed so pleased over these heartening milestones that only a sorehead would ask the question: *What took so long?*

E.R.A., which would not be needed if the sexes were, indeed, treated equally, has still not been ratified by the requisite number of states (38 states are required; 35 state legislatures have voted the act into law and five that had ratified it chose to rescind it). In the United States Senate, there is one woman among 103 male senators. And as we go to press, no woman has ever yet been appointed to the United States Supreme Court.

At the topmost levels of business, where women are occasionally ensconced in highly visible positions (largely in response to government and/or social pressures), the female executive so elevated does not enjoy the same corporate perks as her male counterparts, does not pack comparable executive clout, and does not take home the same size paycheck. Her value is, indeed, less to the company because she does not have equal opportunity to contribute.

Executive women have little or no voice in the big, hard-core corporate decisions and most of them have entered into a kind of weird conspiracy with management to make it appear that they really do. Why would women become willing players in such a charade? Easy. They're embarrassed to be tokens and feel that pretending not to be may (a) impress someone important, and (b) help them get a genuine executive position somewhere else, where they'll be allowed to use the talent and training they are not permitted to use now.

Who's to blame for all this?

They are—the men!—cries many a frustrated woman, and the cry is, of course, understandably credible. After all, the men are running the show. Still, women must be doing something wrong. Or there must be something they could be or should be doing differently.

You bet there is! Plenty. The old, old-fashioned ideas that are keeping women in the "kitchens" of business can be changed. They are, in fact, changing now, and this book is meant to help speed up the switch. It will explore the male-female attitudes that underlie and reinforce the inequities in business and cite the things women do that provide management with the chalk to draw the line on their participation in the more meaningful corporate functions. It's a delicate line, often barely perceptible or even invisible, but it *is* drawn. And beyond it women are not only unwelcome in most businesses, they are subtly but summarily barred.

The best thing that's happened to business in this century is the influx of women and their availability for jobs above the traditional levels of secretary and clerk. Still, there are elements of tradition that continue to hold both sexes in a deadly embrace, killing the men and turning the women into malcontents.

The quality is down and the prices are up on virtually everything and one big reason for this is that there simply aren't enough capable, caring people at work in the key areas of the companies that produce the goods and services. We keep telling ourselves and each other this, but if anyone is listening, nobody is doing enough about it. Tradition keeps supercapable women tied to chimpanzee chores while pushing so-so men into stressful situations where the demands are beyond their performance levels. It's no favor to a man to move him into a job he can't hack, no matter how much he wants the money to support an able-bodied woman who would probably be much happier—and better company —if she had the pleasure of supporting herself.

BBDO—industry shorthand for Batten, Barton, Durstine, and Osborne, the giant advertising agency headquartered in New York—did a survey at the end of 1979 on male attitudes toward women across the country. Men aged eighteen to fifty were interrogated in twenty cities and, according to Niki Scott of the United Press Syndicate, this is what surfaced:

Eighty percent want their women to be, more than anything else, good mothers, and while 82 percent declared that they approve of working mothers, 59 percent admitted they'd rather not work with a woman. (That's *with*, never mind *for*—which the study conductors apparently would rather not get into.) Among the married men questioned, 75 percent said that the major responsibility for cooking dinner was the wife's; 80 percent leave her all the dirty laundry; and 78 percent think that cleaning the bathroom is her job.

The men expressed preference for female company when dining out, having cocktails, and discussing personal problems but opted for "the boys" when they want to talk politics or take in sports either as players or spectators. They see women as more intelligent, more self-confident, more ambitious, and more aggressive than they used to be and think the change is for the better—in spite of the fact that they also believe today's women are less family oriented and less faithful to their husbands.

The survey also revealed that the classic "male chores" around the house are still male. Sixty-three percent of the men said they do all the drink mixing, 86 percent are responsible for all household repairs, and 82 percent take out the garbage.

Karen Olshan, vice-president and manager of special projects in the research department for BBDO, was "discouraged" by the survey's findings. "What we learned," she said, "is that change takes a long time to happen. Living in the New York City area, you begin to think that women's liberation has been more effective than it's been."

Yes, Karen, yes!

I recently returned from a tour of the United States that took me from New York to Philadelphia and down the Atlantic seaboard to Washington, Atlanta, Charleston, and Miami; crisscrossing the Sunbelt to New Orleans, Baton Rouge, Houston, Dallas/Fort Worth, Memphis, and Nashville; through the Midwest to Chicago, Cleveland, Detroit, Saint Louis, Minneapolis, and, farther, to Denver; then, finally, to Seattle, Portland, San Francisco, and Los Angeles. All over the country the story is the same. Women are literally pouring into the work force. You can see them in the early morning—an army of well-educated, well-dressed females swinging out of the house carrying expensive "designer" briefcases. Their brisk step and cheery, determined expressions are reminiscent of the young men of the fifties and sixties who are now running the business world—or sweating out disappointing careers until time for retirement.

In New York they disappear down the subway stairs, clamber onto the bus, or hail a cab. In other cities most of them hop into brand-new compact cars, the new working woman's status symbol, which will be stashed for the day in parking garages or lots near the job. These career women are "good for business" in more ways than one, a shot in the arm to the economy with their earnings as well as with their know-how, skills, and ambition.

Unfortunately, business appears to be more interested in attracting the earnings than in making optimum use of the know-how, skills, and ambition; or, to put it more bluntly, more interested in raking the re-

wards in than dishing them out. There is a stampede to
sell the career woman everything known to God, man,
and the manufacturer. Suddenly she is the target of all
the hyped-up reverence that Procter & Gamble has
heaped on the career housewife for sixty-five years. Virtually every advertising campaign must take some note
of her, and as this is written, there are no fewer than
eight magazines devoted exclusively to her. Meanwhile
other old faithfuls such as *Mademoiselle, Vogue, Glam-
our,* and *Harper's Bazaar* are heavily weighted toward
her interests (or what their editors and publishers believe her interests to be).

At the same time there is a genuine backlash against
this New Woman. Career housewives fear and resent
her as the potential asp at the office. Male co-workers
suspect and resist her because they are perceiving her,
for the first time, as a worthy competitor who must be
stopped before she becomes a serious contender for the
jobs they're shooting for.

In Detroit an angry woman in the television audience
sprang out of her seat during the question-and-answer
segment of the John Kelly show, where I was a guest,
and expressed her resentment: "My husband is a sales-
man," she said, "and his company has hired a woman to
sell with him. Right now they're on the road together,
flying around the country on the same airplanes and
staying in the same hotels. She's twenty-eight years old
and good-looking and he's a man and only human and
I'm back here at home, tied to three kids and worried
sick!"

In Minneapolis an equally angry man said to me,
"Don't get me wrong, I believe it's okay for women to

work if they want to; I just don't want to think I've got to compete with them. It isn't quite fair—for them or for us either. The government's on their side but management, thank God! is still on ours. It's okay for them to be secretaries and office workers because everybody's used to them in those jobs, but when they start getting into other things, it creates problems."

I'm afraid I made the irate Detroit woman even madder by remarking that her husband might be worried sick about what she is doing while he's away from home (one assumes that whatever arrangements she made for care of the three children while she was at a television studio participating in a "live" show would work the same for a romantic rendezvous). I reminded her that her husband didn't have to get out of town to get mixed up in a bit of hanky-panky if he's so inclined, or to encounter temptation in that direction either.

As for the Minneapolis man, I quietly pointed out to him that there was a time not long past when business wasn't ready for women in any capacity, and the idea that they "don't belong" in executive positions makes no more sense than his great-grandfather's notion that women couldn't handle office correspondence or keep books.

It is interesting to note that quite a few men who earnestly wish that career women would go home and stay there are now making a conspicuous show of generosity toward them in an effort to prove that they are plugged into the new thinking. This is particularly true of the aging men in middle management who are afraid they may appear to be "uncontemporary" or (God forbid!) old and out of it, even candidates for early retirement.

Those closet dissenters are the ones to watch out for, and the very ones who can be most damaging to the career of a young woman at the outset. The men in middle management have been called the most unprotected group in the country and, therefore, the most discontented and most dangerous. They will fight tooth and nail for their own turf, which they are prepared to defend against all comers—regardless of race, creed, or national origin. Or sex. They are weary of competing with the bright, ambitious young men and now—give a look!—here come the girls!

Women have a lot to learn about business and the very first item is that it is not enough to do a job well or even brilliantly. You've got to "fit in," and for a woman trying to make her way in a man's world, this is not a bit easy. As the song goes, "You've Got to Know the Territory"—where the quicksand is, where the pavement is, which are the dead ends leading noplace, and which are the rocky roads leading only to places that nobody in her right mind would really want to go. Above all, which are the high-speed expressways and how one can get there and stay there without being run over.

It's a matter of being alert, sensitive to the emotional climate and constantly shifting focus of every work situation. It's also a matter of making a place for yourself, fitting yourself into the going "game plan," and finding your own way to get whatever it is you want out of a given job. Men have to do this, too, and while it is (except in cases of government or family intervention) easier for them, it's still no snap. It just seems that way by comparison.

It hardly needs repeating that everybody makes mistakes, and if you aren't making your share, it doesn't follow that you are admired as a lofty perfectionist or some kind of freaky paragon who is always right. It may mean that you're not doing enough. Top management is results oriented and action prone. It expects you to get things done and that means doing a lot. That, in turn, means making mistakes. Some of them are avoidable and amendable and this book will suggest ways to sidestep and correct them. Others are much more serious, defying solution. But ridding ourselves of the first group will make it easier to cope realistically and effectively with the second.

It should be observed up front that the pitfalls under discussion here do not apply exclusively to women. While some of them are particularly "female" pitfalls, men blunder into most of them, too. Men are more likely to get away with them, however, because men are part of the terrain, not looked upon as interlopers who must prove their right even to be there, and not prejudged by gender. It should also be observed that the men who occupy the seats of real power and glory either don't make these mistakes at all or don't compound them by repetition—at least until they have risen high enough to engage in cavalier conduct unforgivable in underlings.

Corporate America has been under fire as long as it has been there, and during the sixties and seventies the sniping escalated into bombardment. Consumerism became an industry, providing election issues for politicians, fame for people who otherwise might have gone unnoticed, and tons of material for the media.

Although the fuel shortage and inflation appear to be

deflecting flak from consumerism, it is still fashionable to malign and vilify Big Business as the progenitor of all our woes, quite as if it didn't underwrite everything we profess to treasure, including our noblest arts and sciences. That thieves and bastards flourish throughout the business world is beyond any doubting, and if more of them are there than anyplace else, it's only because more of everything is there. Is this anyplace for a woman? That is no longer the question, since the new economic squeeze is demanding all hands, all heads for survival. Dour, sour Calvin Coolidge wasn't far off the mark when he announced that "The business of America is business." If a more popular President had said it, this terse little sentence might be embroidered on our samplers and emblazoned on office plaques.

There has been too much make-believe about women in business, too much hocus, inadvertent and planned. It's time to shuck the pretenses on all sides and deal with the hard realities. If you are going to swap your time for money, you should take the steps necessary to make the exchange profitable for yourself—remembering that time is your most precious asset. Others, of course, are concerned with how you use it but no one so deeply and completely as you.

We are absolutely equal in terms of time alone, yet we know for sure that some people get more out of theirs than others—and therein lies the key to that vaunted executive washroom. The purpose of this book is to help you get the clout as well as the key. As matters stand now, women simply don't have it, even when they're the company showpiece—the elaborately officed, titled, and paid symbol of corporate humanism.

In my opinion, business is the most fun there is—when you win. And as a woman, you win not only by working diligently, effectively, visibly, but by making your work and yourself acceptable to the male business establishment. You have to learn how to function in the existing system, which can shift and turn without notice—and which is made by and for men anyway.

This may not seem right or fair, but if you have chosen to follow a career, there's no point in squandering time and emotional energy brooding about what ought to be. You've got to deal with what *is*—the reality men live by. It's their turf.

Nowhere
to Go but Up

The first step toward getting what you want out of business is knowing what it is. That sounds idiot simple and it ought to be. Yet I talk to dozens of superbright, energetic women who are on fire to accomplish something in the wonderful world of commerce but don't have the foggiest idea what it is, what it could be, or how to go about finding out.

They have formed no goals because they honestly aren't sure about anything: what they can do, what they ought to do to make the most money and derive the most satisfaction, or how to prepare themselves for the larger, more rewarding roles now within their reach.

Some of them are still in school, some are just out and looking around in an effort to discover what's available. Most have been working for a few years but feel they're in a rut. Of course they *are* in a rut if they aren't

moving up in salary and status, and a rut has been
described, a shade too graphically perhaps, as a shallow
grave. All of them know about the time-honored accomplishments of men in the marketplace. Now they
keep reading and hearing about the meteoric rise of
women and are champing at the bit for a piece of the
action. They just aren't a bit certain about which one.

Fairly typical was a young woman who told me that
she has a good job as a manufacturer's representative in
Dallas. "But," she said, "I want a career, not just a job."
("A career, not a job" is another of those clichés that
have had a long, hard ride in the media.)

"I don't want to stay where I am but I really don't
have any strong, preconceived ideas about what I'm
going to do next," she said. "I just know that I want it
to be something Important and Meaningful. I would
also like for it to be something that involves working
with People, which is what I like about the job I've got
now. I meet lots of different People and I enjoy that
because I love People. I would like to do something
that Helps them. I, of course, would like to make some
Real Money, too!" (The capital letters were in her
voice and she could not have been more sincere or more
uncertain.)

Paradoxically, the new opportunities for women have
actually compounded the problem. Now that more
doors are open to them, choosing is confusing—not un-
like facing the distorted apertures in the fun house, but
certainly no barrel of laughs. Which are the revolving
doors, the phony entrances, the fast exits? And how
does one tell the difference between these and the gate-
ways to glorious rewards?

Today's ambitious and determined women are serious about their careers and careful about their decisions, but goal setting is, if anything, more difficult now than it was ten years ago when the opportunities were dimmer. It is infinitely easier to pick an ice cream flavor when the choices are vanilla, chocolate, or strawberry than when twenty-four others are added and changed weekly.

One reason women still have tremendous difficulty making up their minds is that many of them have grown up believing that the acceptable choices for them were, and would always be, extremely limited. They believed that if they dared break the classic female pattern to pursue a nontraditional ambition, they would face overwhelming if not unbeatable odds, to say nothing of unpleasant social consequences, the latter ranging from mild disapproval or pity to hostility and none-too-subtle ostracism. It is difficult for some women to accept the fact that all this is changing now, along with the rest of the world.

This causes them to remain undecided and uncommitted, a condition which can be, and often is, damning to the entire sex—another hurdle for career women who *are* solidly decided and committed. The men in management, and some disillusioned female executives, too, are leery that even the most enthusiastic and promising woman on the premises will drop everything and go strolling off into the sunset with the first appealing man who makes her an offer she can't refuse. Or that she will become pregnant and be lost to the firm in the middle of a crucial program, if not forever.

Unfortunately, the record bears out this belief often

enough to keep the suspicion refueled. The biological facts in the matter are as immutable as they are undeniable and remain the single most significant factor in the role of women in business. Needless to say again, if children are had, it's the woman who's going to have them. And in most instances she is the one who will have primary responsibility for their care—at least in the first crucial weeks. If she and management and her husband have agreed that she is to keep her job, there are problems to be solved. And even though there may be a ready solution, there is always the possibility that her own attitude will undergo some subtle or very clear and obvious changing.

The vice-president of a Boston management consulting firm, a woman who employs a number of well-educated young people of both sexes, recently told me this:

"Most of the young women I've hired have been outstanding. They have excellent taste and perception—and are very good at handling the ego problems of the young male executives we deal with. But I've noticed a marked difference between them and the young men in my department. When the men get married, they work harder to get their marriages off to a good start, to get their households established on a stable basis. When a baby arrives, they work still harder because they have another mouth to feed.

"On the other hand, newlywed women tend to turn their attention away from the job and focus more on their husbands and social activities with other young marrieds. And when they have a baby, the job interest wanes even more.

"I'm deeply concerned right now that one of our junior executives who is out on maternity leave won't come back after the three months we agreed on, even though she was adamant about keeping her job and quite insistent that we hold it for her. It burdens the rest of the staff but we were all very glad to fill in for her because she's a super girl—extremely able and popular. Now, however, when I talk with her on the phone, I can tell that she's less and less interested in what's going on at the office and has hinted twice that she may not be coming back to work after all. Maybe that's as it should be, but she was so emphatic about not wanting to drop her career and her belief that these job activities would actually make her a better mother!"

The female executive who was telling me this can empathize completely because she is married and has two grown-up children. She has lived the whole scenario and knows about the ambivalence firsthand.

The young woman involved has a good working relationship with her boss and the two of them have talked about it frankly and openly, which is the only intelligent way to deal with the matter. Secretiveness on either side would be damaging to all concerned—and to the department.

"I feel asinine about it," the new mother says. "But I have to admit that this hasn't turned out the way I expected. I thought I'd just have a baby that I'd stay home and take care of for three months. Then I'd turn the daytime detail over to a good nurse and go back to my job. But it isn't working out that way. I found a really great nurse I wouldn't be a bit queasy about leaving Timothy with. But the point is that I don't want to leave him at all. I'm still nuts about the job I have and get a sinking feeling every time I think about resigning. But I also get a sinking feeling when I think about not being at home with Timothy all day. The nurse could do everything for him that he needs, but I guess it boils down to the need *I* feel to do all those things myself.

"My husband and I have talked about it and I can tell he'd be pleased for me to be home with the baby, but there's this: we need my salary, now more than ever. Also, leaving my salary out of it, I know he's sincere when he says he's afraid that I'll get restless and resentful after a few months. He knows I enjoy the excitement and stimulation of the office and it's wonderful that he understands. But I have to admit I do a deep burn when I think about the fact that he doesn't have to choose between being a father and having a career. I *mind* that he doesn't have to make the choice!"

The immutable biological role of women is, of course, a major consideration in company planning, and we are all kidding each other or ourselves when we pretend that it isn't. Regardless of legal and social pressures to treat women at work equally, management *does* take gender into consideration when people are employed or promoted, because any sensible management must. (This, in spite of the fact that study after study has shown that young men are much more likely to leave a company than young women.) Female gender will always be nagging away at some mental corner of any employer, man or woman, at decision time, and while we may protest at the unfairness of it all, the situation is not changed. Never mind what is right or fair. We are concerning ourselves here with reality and how to cope with it until the government or the companies themselves have found satisfactory solutions.

Any woman with far-reaching career ambitions must deal with her own biology and emotional makeup along with her mentality and training. She has to make some hard choices: to marry or not, to have children or not, to stay home and devote a lot of years to full-time mothering or turn the job over to servants or (if she's lucky) an available, willing, and inexpensive relative. If she's elected marriage and motherhood, her career goals naturally must be adjusted to fit. The fact that men do not have to make the choices or the adjustments is something we may damn as an unfair or even an exploitative advantage—but we cannot change it. Railing away at the biological inequity of it all is only a waste of time and emotional energy.

Kelly, who, at age thirty, has worked her way up at CBS in New York and now heads a key department, is in an agony of indecision about having children. "I've been married four years," she said, "and I keep putting off pregnancy because I like my job so much. I've moved ahead fast here and I'm afraid if I take time out, it will interrupt my progress. CBS has a very liberal policy for women. If I leave to have a baby, I'll go with a guarantee of a job at the same level when I come back. Of course, they can't guarantee me the *same* job that I left. The company has to keep operating and respecting the ambitions of other people—which I understand. But you see what I mean? The job I get when I come back from maternity leave may be in an area I don't like as much or that won't offer me as much opportunity. Every time I go to the gynecologist, I ask,

'Are you sure I can still have a baby a couple of years from now?' And nearly every day I ask myself, 'Are you sure all this is worth it—not having children, I mean?' I guess I want to have my cake and eat it, too. . . ."

Having one's cake and eating it, too, may be selfish but the desire is certainly universal. Although nobody will ever figure out a way to do that, it is possible to figure out ways to balance the layers of the cake between ownership and consumption. Business follows systems and while the systems often don't make sense, they do make the rules. The object is to make the systems work for you, to get what you want in exchange for your time, skills, intellect, and effort. It can happen. But it takes planning. Goal setting.

Deciding what you want becomes easier when you examine the choices in terms of your own motivations:

1. *Money.* There is no point in chewing over all the old saws about *that*, because money is why most people work. Love of the stuff may or may not be at the root of all evil, but it is, without question, at the root of most effort. It is, again without question, the main reason why the percentage of adult women at work outside the home passed the halfway mark in 1979 and continues upward. That second income in the household is no longer just wanted, it is actively needed.

2. *Power.* At least one of my female colleagues defines power as money, but I have known so many people who had one without the other that I cannot agree. During the so-called Women's Revolution, I have seen at least a dozen women ensconced

in positions that commanded dazzling salaries and corporate perks but not the faintest whisper of a voice in any high-level corporate decision. One friend told me "in graveyard confidence" that she is paid $78,000 a year, ostensibly heads a staff of thirty-one people, and enjoys an enviable cluster of company benefits (insurance, child education, medical program, retirement plan, the works—all maximum and deluxe), yet does not exercise real control over her department and is virtually ignored in the high-level meetings she attends. How come? "I am there as a symbol of 'corporate humanism,' to prove that my company is hewing to the government guidelines and laws in regard to minorities. Also, I'm good publicity. Seventy-eight thousand plus the cost of perks may sound like a whole lot to pay a symbol, but it's peanuts to a billion-dollar-a-year corporation—a small price to pay to keep the government and special interest groups off their backs."

A few female executives do have genuine clout, but it remains a rare thing, regardless of talent, training, dedication, or anything else. Obversely, there are a number of men around who hold positions of enormous power but eke out a meager living from them. Still, the real power *is* vested in men, almost 100 percent. But that doesn't keep women from wanting it or searching for ways to get it.

3. *Ego Gratification.* Women have always enjoyed being admired for their beauty, charm, social graces, and many-splendored accomplishments as hostesses and homemakers. They still do. Now,

however, they also enjoy recognition as achievers in business. "Look," Kelly said to me, "I'm crazy about making the money I do—which is almost as much as my husband is making and more than my dad is getting out of his business. That's gratifying to me. But I have to admit that my job is an ego thing, too. I get a real charge out of being head of a whole department in a big, glamorous industry and having people know it." Kelly does control her department and does have a voice in major decisions. Aren't some of the women envious, jealous? Aren't some of the men resentful? "Yes," she replies with applaudable candor, "and I guess I have to admit that I get a tingle of satisfaction out of that, too!"

There is enormous ego gratification, too, in the development of a talent—an opportunity that tradition has denied to women if the talent has ranged beyond the welcome mat and the picket fence. Ronnie, an extraordinarily gifted fashion designer, left the small midwestern town where she was born and raised to brave New York's supertough Seventh Avenue because she "had an itch that had to be scratched." Ronnie was under pressure from her family and peers to marry a hometown boy and settle down there. "But I couldn't do it," she said. "Making clothes for myself and children would never have been enough. I'd have been miserable unless I had proved that I can design clothes that would be attractive and workable and satisfying for thousands of women whose needs were going begging."

4. *Fame.* This being the era of the Instant Celeb-

rity, the era when one of our self-declared sages, Andy Warhol, announced that everyone will be famous for fifteen minutes, it is not surprising to see men, women, and very small children chasing headlines, klieg lights, and flash guns with all the fervor of a beagle on speed. Thanks to the advent of new reportorial techniques in print as well as in television, the business celebrity stands front and center, too; not the same object of adulation as, say, a rock star or bonus shortstop, but a bona fide limelight presence nevertheless. Further zing has been provided by the upward mobility of career women, and the celebrity status accorded *them* has caused the new female vice-president who loves applause to stop envying Charlie's Angels.

5. *All of the Above.* Although money, power, ego gratification, and fame are not interchangeable, they do tend to overlap and most of us would happily opt for some of each. It is necessary to decide, however, which of these is the top entice-ment for you and, once you've been honest with yourself about this, the rest is easier. You choose your field, your company, your job there accord-ing to which offers the likeliest opportunity to achieve 1, 2, 3, 4, or some of each. There is nothing really "wrong" with wanting any or all of them, although our literature would be exceedingly poor without the condemnations of each. Self-fulfillment is the respectable ambition to declare out loud, but this warm, happy feeling is usually generated by one of the motivations cited above.

The most successful women I know in business are all "goal oriented" and have programmed their careers to meet firm, clear objectives. Having set them, they have actively pursued them by pitching in and getting whatever expertise it took to reach them. They went after—and got—the knowledge, skills, and experience required for each. Their goals changed as goals must with the march of time and the shifts in circumstance, but always they have kept an objective firmly in mind. When new doors opened, they stepped inside if the view appeared promising; and when doors closed (or were slammed in their faces), they looked about for others. They have also come to terms with themselves and the world about the matters of marriage, divorce, childbearing, homemaking, and socializing.

Paula D. Hughes, who is one of the top ten stockbrokers on every Wall Street list, started her career in New York as a secretary. Anybody can tell you that a secretarial job is the deadest dead end in town, but nobody can tell Paula that. She is multimillion-dollar proof to the contrary.

In the late fifties Paula looked beyond her typewriter for greener pastures, decided there were good opportunities in the advertising field, and conducted a successful campaign to get a job with a giant advertising specialty firm as a sales representative. She was selling ideas, "a lot like selling patches of blue sky," but she quickly reached her first goal there, which was to be Number One in sales. Having always had a healthy interest in money, Paula, while still selling blue sky, turned more and more attention to the stock market. She followed the daily stock reports, learned the language of Wall Street, discovered which sources of information were reliable, and mined those for pointers on analyzing the potential of various stocks and bonds. Then she began to make small-scale investments. Encouraged by profits from these—and entreated by clients to do for them what she was doing for herself—she moved to a brokerage firm. At the time almost no women had ever been admitted into the magic circle. (What? A "customer's man" who is a woman? Who's gonna stand for that?)

Paula ignored the improbability of the situation and steamed ahead. Her first goal as a broker was to open a new account every day, and she would not go home at night until she did. Her next goal was to be the Number One broker in her office and then in her firm, which happened because she made it happen. Then she set her sights on becoming a vice-president. Along the way, she moved to Thomson McKinnon Securities, Inc., where she is now first vice-president and a member of that august firm's board of directors.

Does she have any new goals? Yes. Two. She wants a major corporate directorship outside the brokerage field and an honorary degree, the latter because she didn't go to college! (The paradox is that she is a university trustee.)

How has her career affected Paula's family life? "Mostly positively," she says. She is a divorcée and while she feels that her career did not cause the divorce, she is sure that her successes in business gave her the confidence and courage to get out of an unhappy marriage. She feels, too, that the career helped her happily married daughter grow up to be "a whole person" with the self-assurance and determination to follow her own instincts. "My daughter, Cathy," she adds, "is a 'career dropout' who scrapped an executive position with a university to pot plants for a florist. That's what she wants to do and, by golly, she's got the courage to do it!"

Christy Bulkeley, who is publisher of the Danville, Illinois, *Commercial-News* (one of the "hot" properties of the Gannett chain), speaks feelingly about the importance of keeping options open, being willing to listen to someone else's evaluations of your capabilities and willing to adjust goals accordingly. Christy is the woman to speak. She did not set out to be a publisher. Women have always been about as welcome on the average newspaper as a 20 percent pay cut, and in the sixties, when Christy started, a woman in the top spot would have been unprintable news to the hired help, even if she owned the joint.

What Christy intended to be was a crack political reporter and she prepared herself for this at the University of Missouri, earning a degree there in the School of Journalism. This was before the advent of "Woodstein" and the surge of interest in "investigative journalism" that followed the Watergate exposé.

"I wanted to cover the news at the middle of the bureaucracy where things happen that can be controlled if they're discovered in time. I think the principal problem with government is the lack of communication between the lawmakers and those whom the laws affect. People should know what government is about to do and government should know what the people want done. In my opinion, the primary respon-

sibility of a political reporter is to dig out this information and get it printed."

Christy had been an outstanding reporter on Gannett's Rochester newspapers for eight years when she
became national president of Women in Communications. The organizational and administrative skills she
demonstrated working in previous capacities for WICI
had impressed the Gannett upper echelon, and Al New-
harth there broke one of the most hardened traditions
in the news business by offering her the position of
publisher of the chain's paper at Saratoga Springs. Her
success there won her the job as publisher and president of Gannett's much larger paper in Illinois.

"Now," Christy says, "my job is to provide the resources and the environment for a lot of people to function as I did when I was acting as an individual. It is up
to me to furnish the facilities and create the work climate that will make a whole staff competent enough
and confident enough to push their own skills to the
outer limits instead of retreating into the herd for security."

She makes it sound easy, but publishing a newspaper
requires a delicate balance of skills that are often at
war with each other. She must be both "editorial" and
"administrative," a reporter still passionately concerned
with the news but also that creature reporters abhor,
the boss—and a woman boss at that!

What are her next goals? To refine and enlarge the
publishing resources she presides over. "But," she
quickly adds, "I have not scrapped my plan for gov-
ernment-to-people, people-to-government communication on an individual basis. Right now my goal is to

train, motivate, and strengthen the talents of other news people. But I've got a lot of years ahead of me and eventually I will undertake a large-scale national project on my own." A book? A column? "Yes—to both questions."

Christy was married three years ago, having concentrated her interests and energies on her career during the years when most women are raising families. She is blessed with a writing husband who is generous about her career and helpful in matters of household management.

Kay Lockridge still prefers to be a loner and is happy to have attained the big goal she set for herself when she was "a kid in Indiana." She lives in New York ("where I always dreamed of being, although the thought of the Big Apple, frankly, scared hell out of me") and makes her own schedule as a free-lance writer and editor. Along the way, she paused to fulfill other ambitions: among them, to be an Associated Press reporter and editor ("In Indiana the AP seemed like the loftiest thing in the world and for four years I was one of AP's proudest"); to be a teacher ("It's the ultimate ego trip to have a captive audience, as I did at Michigan State! I had a ball pontificating about all the things I'd learned at the Associated Press"); and to fly a plane ("The day I landed an airplane by myself and realized I hadn't crashed it, I knew I was ready for New York!").

Kay, too, has been attracted to the stock market as a dandy place to augment income ("The freedom in free lance can become a luxury item") and spends an hour or so a day studying the market reports—which is fun for her, she says, but not enough to lure her away from the typewriter.

She prepared herself for a career of writing and editing with a Bachelor of Arts at Miami University in Oxford, Ohio, followed by a Master of Journalism at Syracuse University in New York.

Kay hasn't married because, so far, the men she might choose to share her life with haven't wanted a working wife. Will she? Maybe, someday—who can say? Her ultimate goal: to write an important novel about newspaper people caught between their personal interests and public responsibilities. "Don't tell me," she says, "I know it's been done. But hasn't everything? The trick is to develop a fresh angle and that's what I intend to do."

Most female overachievers set their goals early. Examples of "late-blooming" successes do abound, but there's no telling how much more abundant the flowering would have been if they had made earlier decisions.

One of the more admirable early goal setters is Esther Coopersmith in Washington. Esther says she decided at age seventeen that "to get what you want in the world you must either have money or be able to raise it. I didn't have any. My parents were both immigrants struggling to make a living under some rather discouraging handicaps. My mother, for instance, spoke four other languages but no English.

"Since I had no money, I decided to learn how to raise it. I worked hard at the University of Wisconsin and after graduating cum laude went to Washington and got a job with Estes Kefauver in his presidential campaign. He asked me to come to Washington from

Wisconsin because at age seventeen I had been chairman of a fund-raising dinner where he had been the speaker." Esther became a planner and project manager in fund-raising for the organizations and individuals engaged in politics and charitable causes. She met presidents, senators, and other important people whose opinions influence key decisions in business and government. She is now recognized as one of the nation's finest fund-raising specialists.

Esther has developed a kind of social grace that makes her the ultimate Washington hostess, the town's most likely successor to the redoubtable Perle Mesta. She is the kind of woman who doesn't hesitate to get the Arabs and Jews together at a terrace barbecue—a feat she engineered while Sadat and Begin were pow-wowing with the President at Camp David. As this is written, she is the Numero Uno fund raiser for the Democratic Party, has been a recent delegate to the United States mission at the United Nations, and is heading a project to raise sorely needed millions for the museum at Cairo, where some of the world's all-but-priceless treasures are receiving less than cherished care.

Esther is happily married and the mother of four overachieving children who enjoy their mother's public role. To accommodate home, hearth, and family, she has conducted her career on an in-and-out basis, soft-pedaling business interests when the need for her at home was great and escalating them at times when the need slackened. Fortunately, the Coopersmiths can afford an excellent household staff, which she quickly credits with "keeping things together."

Getting what you want out of business does not necessarily involve grand-scale ambitions. Katie Thompson recently retired from her job as counselor in the Baton Rouge school system with a lifelong pension —at the ripe old age of forty-one. Almost simultaneously she remarried and has now moved to Radford, Virginia, where her husband is an engineer and a "sideline farmer." Katie has a new counseling job at a school in Radford, which does not interfere with her pension from Louisiana.

"My daughter, Taralyn, was still a baby when I divorced," she said, "and providing for her was my main concern. My mother, brother, and I all had houses in the same neighborhood and I could count on Opal (my mother) and Celeste (my brother's wife) to baby-sit for me. I had a good job as counselor in one of the Baton Rouge high schools and when Taralyn was old enough to go to school, her hours there were about the same as mine, although my students often had problems that kept me late. Anyway, I was able to earn a good living and at the same time give Taralyn the attention she needed and that I enjoyed.

"I had no ambition at all to move up in the school system, although I could have. Several times I was urged to apply for bigger jobs that opened up and somebody was always suggesting that I go to summer school or night school at L.S.U. (which was right across town) and get a Master's or a Ph.D. That just wasn't what I wanted to do. I didn't want to get involved in school politics and I preferred spending my spare time with Taralyn. Besides, I knew I'd marry again when the right man came along and he finally did. The timing was perfect! We postponed the wedding until school was out and I became eligible for twenty-year retirement."

Katie made the system work for her, getting out of it exactly what she wanted: a good, steady income from a job that gave her almost as much time with her daughter as she would have had if she had not been working. And now a monthly paycheck that is no fortune, but a welcome extra for the rest of her life.

Her next goal? "Now that nobody is nagging me to do it," she said, "and there's no university ten minutes away, I think I'll start working on my Ph.D. Taralyn will soon be grown up and my husband wants me to do as I please. That makes two of us! So far, I've managed to get what I wanted from my work—which was a comfortable living for the two of us. Now it will be fun to find out what I can accomplish that will be rewarding for all of us!"

One of the women I know who has had difficulty setting a goal for herself is Kim Scott Redmond, who found herself in a depressing quandary when divorce made it unexpectedly necessary for her to earn a living for herself and toddler son, Zoli. Kim had elected marriage instead of college. She had been an indifferent high school student, one of those gorgeous girls much in demand for dating and partying. A divorcée at twenty-three, she had no advanced education and no work experience beyond a brief fling at fashion modeling.

She feels that fashion modeling is too short-lived and chancy to offer a dependable livelihood for herself and her son. She says that she collects no alimony, gets limited child support, and realizes that she will have principal responsibility for Zoli's upbringing and education—must prepare somehow to do it.

What can she do? Nothing—she thought. What does she like? Fashion, clothes. How can she earn a living on a penchant as vague and tenuous as that? Kim went to the Johnson O'Connor Research Foundation for aptitude testing in an effort to find some direction for a productive and agreeable career. The test revealed an unusually high aptitude for management that nobody had suspected she harbored—especially Kim, who up until then had felt she couldn't manage anything, including her own life. The counselors at Johnson O'Connor suggested that since she enjoys clothes, she should get a degree in business administration from the Fashion Institute of Technology and apply for a management job in the retail industry, where there is a growing demand for capable people—and a growing shortage of them. She has enrolled at F.I.T. and now feels good about the future because, for the first time, she feels good about herself.

"I never had a terrific opinion of myself in the brain department," she said, "because I got low grades in school on all those things I didn't like. Now I'm into something that excites me and because I like it, and, at the same time, have discovered where my real abilities are, things are entirely different for me. Because I know where I'm going now, I'm not afraid to open up and go!"

Kim has her goal now. She intends eventually to be the chief operating officer of a large fashion store or chain of stores. She hopes to start as an assistant man-

ager of a department in a large store—or in an overall
capacity in a small store. She expects to become a manager within two to four years and move up or move on
from there.

Women's goals and the reasons behind them are as
varied as women themselves. Now that female ambition
has become respectable, you don't have to be a latter-
day Hetty Green to want money, a Bloody Mary to
crave power, a Cinderella to long for ego gratification, or
a Divine Sarah to bask in your industry's version of fame.
The most successful women I know have attained an
enjoyable amalgam of all four but, like the men, few
are willing to admit that their major motivation is anything so worldly as money or power or fame. They are
right. The desire to be as good as you can for as long as
you can is still the most applaudable ambition. Whatever yours may be, whether you plan to work for a few
years, or till you drop dead, or until some crisis in your
life has blown over, here are some things to remember:

1. *Set yourself some firm, clear goals.* Have an
overall objective and, within that, intermediate
goals, with a reasonable timetable for each. The
overall objective can be—and perhaps should be
—a dream as big as the Ritz. But be sure the intermediate goals are realistic and attainable. Reaching
one of the magic markers is not only cheering, it
steams you up to go charging on toward the next
one.

2. *Don't broadcast them.* Make your goals emphatically known to management, where ambition
is admired and appreciated, but otherwise keep

them to yourself. Your peers (more's the pity!) may make you uncomfortable about them. They may even dig in to try to convince you that you're overambitious and that you're making yourself look ridiculous—a handy way to discourage you while they pursue the same prize themselves. Also: please be careful not to offend the older women on the premises who worked their way along slowly and painfully without the aid and comfort of today's more receptive attitudes and equal opportunity laws. These women bear honorable battle scars and the last thing they need is a young smart-ass next door, advertising her intent to become a vice-president in six months, two years, or whatever.

3. *Get the training you need to pursue your goals,* because it still isn't easy for anybody. Get it quickly, as soon as you possibly can. Being a woman in the middle of this media-charged Women's Movement doesn't mean that you'll be swept along by the winds of revolution—although there are men around who bitterly think so. Being male has not been enough for them; being female will most certainly not be enough for you, no matter how many laws are passed or how much social pressure is brought to bear.

4. *Check your track record at intervals* to see how your goals and timetable are matching up. If they aren't, examine the reasons why—and if the reasons aren't good and sufficient, consider the options: whether you should change jobs, change goals, or change the way you're doing things.

5. *If you've been working without firm, clear goals, don't make the mistake of assuming that it's too late now.* It never is. Try. Could be that you're irrevocably stymied where you are, but who says you have to stay? Who says you can't reshape your life? If anybody does tell you that, don't listen. The only opinion that really counts is your own. We all have unlimited resources and you don't know what you can do until you try.

Hands Off

3

The Best Operators Are the Best Delegators

Put those words to music and there you have it: the beginning of a national business anthem.

Watch the men around you chop up a job, no matter how small it may be already, and parcel out the pieces. Even though it may be quicker and easier to do the whole thing themselves, they hand off bits of it here and there for a variety of interesting reasons: maybe because they don't know how to do one part or another, maybe because they realize that Tom, Dick, or Harriet can do it better. More likely, they rid themselves of these chores because the details are either unimportant, professionally risky, or something they just don't like to do.

The next step is to ride herd on the assignees, as-

suring them that what they're doing is vital but really
no big deal. ("Hey, Tom baby, you got that little thing
finished, yet? Two-hour job, but a bottleneck for the
whole project till it's done. Let's crack into it—fast—
okay?") At the same time the shrewd delegator drama-
tizes the project to top management as Götterdämmer-
ung material. ("Hello, Mr. Wormwood, sir—this one
turned out to be an incredibly complex monster, but
not to worry. My team is on the case—and we'll have
the whole thing worked out in two weeks, max.") Step
three, of course, is to bring all the completed parts together into one big finished product and take credit for
all of it!

Women, on the other hand, tend to hang onto every
detail of an assignment, even though it's overwhelm-
ingly huge and complicated. A woman who is the
newly appointed head of research for a large insurance
company told me this: "I know I should turn more responsibility over to my staff but, to tell you the truth,
I'm afraid to! It isn't that I don't trust the people in my
department. Most of them really know their business
and several are outstanding. It's just that I feel so *responsible*...."

This woman is not alone in her sensitivity to what is
expected of her and what she expects of herself on her
new job. Women do feel inordinately responsible for
work that is under their jurisdiction and "take it hard"
when anything goes wrong. Aware as they are that it is
not standard operating procedure to give female employees positions that really matter, they can easily
"freeze" to an assignment, becoming emotionally unable to let any part of it go. Women who do this are

afraid that if a detail is botched, neglected, or overlooked, they'll get full blame for the breakdown regardless of the circumstances. Could be, too, since top
management may just as easily assume that the foul-up
occurred because a woman was in charge. (Has an error
ever been attributed to the gender of a man? Possibly.
But not likely.)

This is not to suggest that women are infallible but
dumped on while men are irresponsible but get away
with it. It is interesting, however, that when something
goes wrong at work, most men are able to take it in
stride. They have an emotionally healthy way of accepting the fact that a certain amount of error is in-
evitable and they will comment almost breezily, "Well,
we blew that one, didn't we?" Women, under similar
circumstances, seldom shrug the matter off as something *we* blew. To the female involved, it's something *I*
did wrong and she will heap guilt on herself by the
carload—meanwhile resolving to keep a tighter grip on
things in the future. Women feel more vulnerable and
this makes it difficult for them to turn over parts of the
work at hand to someone else.

Barbara Smith is one of the best delegators extant, a
vice-president and management supervisor at Ogilvy &
Mather, the well-known advertising agency. Three account supervisors and two account executives report to
Barbara, who follows the dictum that is all but tattooed
onto the anatomy of Ogilvy & Mather executives: *"If
you want to grow, you've got to let go."*

Barbara says this: "I think the difficulty some executives experience in delegating may stem from the fact
that they began as craftsmen. It's hard to graduate

from *doing* to *reviewing*, and when you're going over
the work of a subordinate—the kind of work you've
been doing very successfully yourself—it often seems
easier to pitch in and revise it personally than to suggest revisions and stand back while the person responsible makes them. Actually it's demeaning to another human being to take over his or her work and do
it yourself, and doing this may guarantee that you'll
have to keep it up. Appropriating the job will deprive
the other person of valuable experience in working out
problems, and that, in turn, will deprive you of the
seasoned help you need to extend your own effectiveness."

Contrast that with the methods of a young executive
woman I know at another ad agency who says, "I don't
have time to sit and explain small things to an employee when I can do them myself in my sleep. It
would take longer for me to tell somebody else how to
handle little details in my division than it takes me to
just go ahead and do it. I expect the people who work
for me to catch on by watching me and then studying
what I did."

Barbara smiles knowingly at that and says, "She's
right about the time but only at the moment. Not in the
long run! It takes time at first, but taking a few minutes
to explain and suggest develops problem solvers who
can be genuinely useful. That's a lot better than being
surrounded by 'hired hands' or 'warm bodies'! The more
they grow, the more helpful to you they become. They
develop the self-confidence necessary to turn in an outstanding performance, and that makes you look good!
When you take their work away and do it yourself, they

don't learn as quickly or as well (if at all), and unless they're supercharged self-starters, they become discouraged and stop trying."

The United States Navy, in its continuing program to develop superior officers, stresses the importance of delegating work. The ability to do this is cited as a major mark of leadership. Navy officers are constantly reminded "to get subordinates to take responsibility, match people and jobs, balance (each) person's needs with task requirements to optimize performance, monitor and follow up results of actions, to be sure tasks are completed to standard."

If Barbara Smith were in the Navy, she would be a superior officer. The people who work with her praise her ability to do all these things with calm assurance and are especially impressed with her understanding of individual differences. Of this Barbara says, "You have to remember that everybody has strengths and weaknesses, regardless of rank, even the people you work for. You learn from the strengths and, at the same time, use your own strong points to shore up any soft spots along the line."

Dr. Dorothy Gregg, who is a corporate vice-president of Celanese and a member of SABET (the Secretary of the Navy's Advisory Board on Education and Training), points out that the organizational principles of American business and those of the military are much the same.

"Corporations," she says, "are paramilitary structures. SABET and Celanese share objectives in education and training and follow them in developing leaders. The leadership qualities nurtured by the Navy are

the same ones sought out and developed by corporations. At Celanese we go to considerable lengths to
identify the fast-track, talented people and direct their
talents and energies into task achievement, skillful use
of influence, management control, counseling, and del-
egation of responsibility. These are the identical objectives of SABET and it would be impossible to over-
emphasize the importance both organizations place on
delegating.

"There are, of course, some necessary differences in
training methods but the end results sought are the
same. What the Navy considers good leadership, corporations consider good leadership—and one of the
most admired qualities is the ability to delegate work
and responsibility to achieve results."

How does Dr. Gregg delegate? Her area of responsibility is corporate communications, a complex and
sensitive area that requires a great deal of time and
attention. Additionally, she is extremely active in industry organizations and consumer affairs as well as
SABET. She is also a public speaker, much in demand
on the heartburn-and-gastritis circuit. Effective delega-
tion is a "must" for her, and she is careful to match
people to projects. Here are two examples:

A thirty-one-year-old chemical engineer who has
worked as a financial analyst and writer in the chemical
field has responsibility for specific areas of the annual
report, which is in some ways the company bible, used
by anybody who wants to know anything about Celanese. He has charge of the report's design and production and, additionally, writes the narrative portions.
Dorothy went through the procedure of preparing and

producing the report with the young man just once. Since that time her involvement with it has been only to go over layouts and copy with him, discussing points on which they may have disagreement or which must be revised in the light of corporate policy. She, of course, also receives progress reports from him at regular intervals and sees final printer's proofs. She can rely on his expertise because his background equips him to understand both the financial and technical elements involved.

Another young man in her department had in-depth experience with a chemical trade publication that permitted him to understand and quickly take over two important projects: *Celanese World*, the in-house publication for all employees, and the Celanese public responsibility report, which goes to a selected list of opinion leaders, delineating Celanese activity in areas of human concern. Again, it was necessary for her to go through production details with him only once.

And how is it possible to turn over such complicated and sensitive assignments to a subordinate after only one run-through? "We maintain detailed, written procedures," she says, "which are, effectively, checklists. This allows a newcomer to catch on quickly and makes it possible for me to let details go with assurance. Naturally, I have total confidence in the ability of both young men to do the work in a superior manner because I have taken care to match their talent and background with the jobs they are expected to do. The procedures, by the way, are constantly updated, often with suggestions from the men themselves. These procedures are so clearly detailed that my own involvement leaves me adequate time to coach my staff for larger roles."

A job similar to Dr. Gregg's crashed around the ears of a woman last summer at a huge oil company in Houston. Sally kept herself so tangled up in the picayune details of the in-house publications that she had no time for the overall planning expected of a director of communications and was remanded to the company's "outplacement department" last summer. In a word, fired. She finally got a job as manager of a publication like one of the five produced in her department at the oil company and now spends the day on the minutiae she couldn't let go, agonizing over typefaces, paper samples, ink colors, comparative price quotes, and story angles that should be left up to the editor. Needless to say, her income crashed along with her status.

Reluctance to delegate responsibility for whatever reason is deadly to a woman's career. It not only limits her effectiveness in the position she occupies, but practically guarantees that she will go no further. If she is frozen to every detail, she is probably overworked already and it becomes obvious that she can't handle any additional assignments because she's got her little hands full now.

I once worked with a woman who was in no way afflicted with reluctance to delegate and she taught me some valuable lessons. She was an empire builder, presiding over the largest creative department in the advertising agency where we both worked. Let's call her Jennifer. Jennifer's secret: "It's easy," she confided. "When a new account comes into the agency, I volunteer immediately to take it on—insisting that my department has the best available talent and experience for the products involved and citing all the background I have that is in any way relevant. Once the account is assigned to my department, I put through an urgent requisition for more art directors and copywriters to work on this new business, pointing out that we have to have more people to give these products the time and attention they need. That's the way to do it! Clamor for the work and then scream for help to get it done!"

The way to do it! Volunteer to take on more responsibility. Ask for it, insist on it, cite all the logical reasons why it should be under your aegis, and then, when it happens, point out the need for more personnel to do an effective job.

Jennifer had studied the *modus operandi* of the men who were moving ahead in the company and had adopted their tactics for herself. Needless to say, she also asked for more money to compensate her for solving all these extra problems for the agency. Most women, however, do not display her zest (or the men's) for acquisition, and that is a resounding mistake. Generally speaking, women remain passive, and passivity in business is not a winner's trait.

Some women not only do not seek out responsibility, they actively resist positions of authority that carry it. They refuse to accept management "plums" because they are convinced they cannot get the kind of support they'll need from others at the company—the same support that might automatically be given to a man in the same job. The president of a chain of stores in New York (where one would expect women to be more aggressive) told me that he tried for several years to re-

cruit a woman manager for one of his stores, concentrating on outstanding women already in the chain's
employ.

Why? "I thought we should have more women in key
jobs," he said. "Over ninety percent of our customers
are women—buying fashions, cosmetics, and household
items. To me it made sense to have women managing
stores, but for a long time I couldn't persuade even one
to take on the responsibility. Finally, after three years
of searching and talking, I found a taker!"

Granted, there have been instances wherein company heads felt "pressured" to employ women in certain key roles and have preprogrammed the refusal—or
the failure of the woman who did accept. I know for
sure, however, that this company president was altogether sincere in his wish to move women into store
management. I talked to the young woman who finally
did take the job and she told me she is happy with her
decision. "I admit I felt funny about it at first. This had
always been a man's job, all over the chain, and I don't
mind telling you I was scared. I really did wonder how
the other people in the store would take it."

How *did* they "take it"? How did they react to getting orders from a woman? "Well, I try not to 'give
orders' or flaunt my authority in any way," she said. "At
first, I guess I bent over backward trying not to do
anything that could be interpreted as 'acting bitchy'
because I knew that's what would be said about me if I
wasn't careful—that I was acting bitchy."

Didn't any of the store employees take advantage of
this low-key approach? "Some tried," she laughed. "You
can always expect that. I had to fire a couple of people

who wouldn't cooperate with me and I suppose they thought that was bitchy. I didn't have any more trouble after that than any manager would expect. I compared notes with the men who manage stores and, of course, they have problems with people who work for them, too. But after those in my store found out I meant business and was as serious about being a real manager as any man, it was okay. I think I get as much respect as the men do because everybody realizes I know what I'm doing and work hard at it. Also, they've learned I'm fair and impartial in the way I treat the people who work for me."

Several other young women who had been reticent about taking on management responsibilities have told me that, once they did it, they discovered it was as FDR said: there was "nothing to fear but fear itself." But in the next breath they admitted they still take care of details that most male managers hand off to underlings and forget about.

The faster-moving male managers (and the women like Jennifer) are usually adept not only at delegating responsibility, but at delegating blame. Remember, they are quick to hand off the parts of a job that are professionally risky as well as the ones they don't like to do or feel that someone else might do better. The parts they hang on to are those that are important enough or visible enough to provide a showcase for themselves.

No matter what goes wrong, if responsibilities have been delegated, it is easy to blame someone else. ("Sorry about that, Mr. Wormwood, sir—we've got a soft spot in the structure that we've been trying to cover. Malabar has a personal problem that everybody's trying to help him through. Especially Jenkins. Guess this proves, though, that Jenkins is wrong in asking me to go along with the setup until Malabar straightens his life out. Certainly hope it isn't necessary to replace them both.")

This may sound exaggerated but it isn't. I actually heard a man who heads the marketing department at one of the great American corporations tell the company president exactly that when one phase of a marketing program bogged down because the marketing manager himself had forgotten to make a phone call. The only changes I made in the quote were the names of Malabar and Jenkins, who, incidentally, were not fired although the president immediately suggested that they should be. It should be added that if the marketing manager had been a woman, the president might have leaped to the conclusion that she was being overprotective of Malabar and Jenkins and, perhaps, was not right for the job. Wouldn't a man be tougher?

Blaming somebody else for one's own mistakes is a despicable trait in either sex and I heartily do *not* recommend that any woman pattern her own actions after those of that reprehensible marketing manager. I repeat the story here only to underline the fact that corporate executives often take drastic measures to shore up their own positions and women must be prepared to cope with a kind of behavior that they didn't learn about in Sunday school.

The decent, effective thing to do is report to Mr. Wormwood in no more than three sentences that the program was momentarily obstructed by the personal problems of an associate too valuable to lose and that

you are getting everything back on the track. You don't
have to be inhuman to be professional, and Mr. Wormwood knows it, no matter how remote he seems.

A good manager delegates the various parts of a job
according to the specific capabilities of available personnel—as the Navy, Barbara Smith, and Dr. Dorothy
Gregg suggest. When she does this, she has time to
concentrate on the overall program. She reviews the
work of each person involved in the assignment, pulls it
all together, and does whatever needs doing to relate it
to "the Big Picture."

Women are often faulted for not seeing "the Big Picture," for thinking small in a way that has nothing to
do with the fabled success of Volkswagen. When I
worked in Philadelphia, I had a redoubtable boss I'll
call Miss Grimsby, who owned one of the most famous
fashion stores in America. She was an acknowledged
fashion authority who dictated to the top designers in
Europe and the United States but was so slavishly devoted to her store ("her baby") that she was there sixteen hours a day, seven days a week. If a carpet needed
to be tacked down, she wanted to see the tack and
wanted to interview the man who was going to hit it
with a hammer. She also wanted to watch while he
struck the blow, all the time shouting instructions and
assuring him he was doing it wrong.

Miss Grimsby was so concerned with "her baby" that
she habitually walked the floor with anxiety about it.
She is the only person I ever knew who literally tore
her hair, yanking out huge handfuls of an ever-thinning
mane—largely in frustration because no one human
being could do all she wanted to do in that store, which

was everything that needed doing. The store promptly tripled in size after she sold it.

In contrast, a male friend of mine runs twenty supermarkets, an association, a buying co-op, and assorted other enterprises from a succession of airplanes and golf courses, visiting all of the premises when and as needed, and relying in the interim on reports from various men and women he has delegated to look after important details. Of course, he is immersed in thinking or planning concerned with one or the other enterprises all the time but he is not wound up like a mummified pharaoh in minutiae.

All of us, to be sure, know people of both sexes who actively enjoy exercising dominion over other people—and exhibiting it, so that all the world may bear witness to their awesome power. In Atlanta a young woman told me that she rejoiced when a woman was recruited to head her department because the man who had preceded her had been "the king of the MCPs."

"He really hated having women around the office in any capacity at all—even as secretaries. Kept telling me the best secretary he ever had was a man and he wished more men would take up typing and shorthand. I thought when we got a woman in here as boss things would be different, but they're not. I guess they're no worse because it wouldn't be possible for them to get worse. But they seem like it because you'd expect a woman to be more considerate. She isn't, though. Doesn't let us do anything except exactly what she says and sits in there all day with her door shut doing everything of any importance herself."

The next day I had occasion to talk to the target of

this criticism and when I asked her how things were going, she said, "Super! I'm having a ball. I know I'm following a tough s.o.b. and it's fun to prove that I can be as tough as he was any day. Nobody can say I'm a shy violet who can be run over—or who can get her job shot out from under her. I'm in total control—and loving it!"

That's a direct quote. I wrote it all down because it struck me as being material suitable for memorialization as Famous Last Words. That same day I met *her* boss and asked how the women are doing in his new "Equal Opportunity Program." He looked dismayed. "Okay, I guess," he said, "but I don't think the women get along with each other too well."

Unfortunately, when a situation like this one develops, top management is inclined to look at it, not as an individual matter, but as a blanket condition, typifying the entire female sex. The observation is, "Women don't get along with each other too well"—not that a particular woman is throwing her weight around.

One of the most successful advertising campaigns ever produced was the series whose theme was "Mother, *please*—I'd rather do it myself!" The television commercial featured mother-daughter disagreements that ended with a firm put-down of maternal authority. The creator of the campaign explains that every little boy and girl yearns for the day when mom's dominance can be escaped and his or her own autonomy can be established.

It is no surprise to see this desire to throw off the old familiar female yoke at the office. Deep down, nobody wants a boss at all, and since our society, by and large, has evolved into a matriarchy (at home), a woman boss can stir up subconscious resentment of the reins Mom held so long. Letting the people who work for you do their jobs—delegating all the responsibility and authority to them that they can handle—can do wonders in heading off this kind of resentment at the gap.

Most reasonable adults would infinitely prefer doing things themselves—particularly the jobs they are being paid to do. The cases that appear to be laziness or elected idleness often come about because the person doing her nails, working the crossword puzzle, or talking to her friends on the telephone has had her duties usurped by someone who is overzealous or overantsy. Allowing an indifferent employee the pleasure of being genuinely useful is a good way to change work habits that are too casual or downright sloppy and unacceptable.

We are, most of us, devastatingly familiar with the corruptive effects of power and, at the same time, tempted. When all your life you've been "just a girl," the temptation to flaunt the power you never thought you'd have may be enormously difficult to resist. Resist it anyway. You can control quietly most of the time, and unless a demonstration becomes absolutely necessary to establish your authority, it's better to be subtle about it. Your employees may knuckle under at the moment but you may discover too late that they're spending more time thinking up ways to get even than producing ideas that will help you get ahead.

Being Lady Tiptop can shut off the flow of creative assistance from people whose help you need. I know women who trap themselves in the minute details of work they have committed to absolute experts—whose expertise is decimated by oversupervision. The hours these women spend in classes, labs, and studios to prepare themselves for their oversupervision would be infinitely more productive for them if they were spent originating new projects that their own capabilities equip them to create and develop. And the work that is being done for them would be infinitely better without their dubious assistance. There is no point in paying premium prices for the work of specialists if you interfere with what they are trying to do for you.

Men, certainly, are known to get in the way of artists and technicians they've recruited. I will never forget the advertising manager who earnestly suggested that the director of a music track being recorded for a television commercial "play it an octave slower." But the insecurity women feel about their positions of authority can cause them to involve themselves needlessly in detail that someone else might very well handle better.

It can help your own career along if you keep these points in mind:

1. *Don't hesitate—delegate! Immediately.* Every time you let something go, you free yourself to accept additional responsibility. Top management is enormously comforted to know that there is a competent person available to take care of new developments. Let it be you.

2. *Follow up.* When you hand off part of an assignment, don't forget it. Without breathing down the neck of the person who's doing the work, make periodic checks by phone and/or memo. It's

not unreasonable to ask for progress reports, although you may encounter a person here and there who thinks so. Just remain calm about it and stay on top of the job.

3. *Keep your superiors informed.* Without breathing down *their* necks, let them know the assignment is under control and proceeding on schedule. This also lets them know that you're a dependable person who's getting things done.

4. *Don't forget to say thank you* when the work you've delegated has been finished and delivered. It's nice to be appreciated—and the people who work for you enjoy a pat on the back as much as you do when your own bosses respond gratefully.

Chapter 4

Giving Up and Giving In...

It is always easier to surrender than to do battle. The struggles of the surrender may, in the long run, be more difficult and demanding and bitter than the abandoned battle, but these are all somewhere down the road, obscured by the merciful mists of the future. For the time being there is a measure of relief in giving up. There is even a sort of heroism in waving a nice white flag, and when waves of applause sweep up from the sidelines in approving answer, the gesture becomes downright gratifying to all concerned, including the one who is making it. Suddenly the disappointment of defeat subsides and the comfort of Fate Accepted sets in. Peace. It's wonderful!

This is often the reaction of women who are making their big move toward, or inside, the job market when they encounter resistance from men, other women, and

management. Women do give up their career ambitions
more readily than men do for a number of valid reasons
—not the least of which is that they can. They're permitted.

A woman knows—or at least thinks she knows—that
she can "always get married" and pass the responsibility for her well-being, financial and otherwise, along to
her legally wedded husband. Society, far from disap-
proving of the switch, will smile upon her for going
along with its most honored tradition and reward her
with lots of fondue pots, barbecue tools, and aprons
imprinted "To Hell with Housework." A man, on the
other hand, knows for sure that unless someone had
both the forethought and wherewithal to leave him a
fortune, he's got to crack into it and work for a living
until he falls in his tracks. It is written into the script
that he must support not only himself but a wife and
children—and in the style somebody has decided they
should become accustomed to. If he reneges in any
way, Society will find a rich variety of ways to embar-
rass him and make him thoroughly uncomfortable
about it.

The marriage option is, perhaps, the single biggest
reason why women scrap their own career plans and
devote themselves to captaining the second team, providing a back-up system for the family breadwinner.
When the going gets rough at work, it can look like an
"easy out." While reams of anguished prose have been
wrung out about the role of working women in the nation's rising divorce rate, very little has been said about
the part played by the "easy out" marriages—i.e., those
entered into by women whose career ambitions have

been frustrated and abandoned. Granted, some marriages undertaken for no better reason do turn out to be
happier and more rewarding for both partners than
anybody had a right to expect. But it is reasonable to
assume that most of them either end up in divorce
court or become reruns of the Thirty Years War. It
hardly takes a Dear Abby to advise women to hold onto
their own goals and hold out for a marriage that is more
than a convenient escape hatch. Yet Abby's mail is a
constant indicator that thousands of women do not.

Married or single, mothers or not, women now com-
prise over half of the American work force but, as previously stated, hold less than 5 percent of the managerial positions. Since all the tests yet devised to
measure human intellect reveal no significant differences between the sexes, something is grossly amiss.
Could it be that more than 96 percent of the women at
work are denied opportunity? Or is it possible that a
substantial number don't recognize it or are not pursu-
ing it? How many have given up?

A young woman I know who did hold out for a
propitious marriage and is still holding on to a career
she enjoys says this: "When Sam and I got married, we
talked about whether I should quit work or not and
decided that it definitely wasn't the thing for me to do.
I work for a national retail chain and the competition for
executive jobs is stiff—from men and other women,
too. I thought women would have an edge at my company because it's concerned mainly with fashion and
home furnishings. But the fellows still get first crack at
the juicy jobs. We have a few women in executive spots
and that's what I'm shooting for. But I get discouraged.

"A man my age who started a few months after I did got the first promotion in our department even though his work isn't as good as mine and our supervisor practically said so. But he knew I was recently married and at the age to be starting a family, and I'm sure that had a lot to do with it.

"When I did become pregnant, Sam and I talked again about whether I ought to quit work but decided we needed the money. I'm glad I went back after the baby came because I like to work and I was lucky to land in another spot that suits me. I'm especially glad when I talk to my neighbors, mostly young women in our suburb who quit their jobs to get married. They're climbing the walls being housewives."

Another woman I know is a $50,000-a-year executive who has chosen not to give up her career but did give up marriage. Still dazzling at forty-one, she says this: "There are, of course, many times when I wish I were married, even though the problems of my friends who *are* married make me feel that it's an overrated institution. It would be nice to have the other comforts and conveniences of marriage I read more about than I see. But I am not going to get married just to prove that I can—or to prove that I am not sexually peculiar or involved with a man I shouldn't be."

Isn't she ever sorry?

"Of course. There are many times when I wish I were married and there have been two times when I almost took the plunge. Honesty compels me to tell you, though, that the times when I almost did were moments of deep discouragement at work. Something had happened to make me feel that a career was just too big a struggle . . . that I might be overambitious and trying to push myself to a job level men don't want women to have.

"Frankly, if the right man had been urging me to give it all up for him at my most despairing moments, I might have acted like one of those career women in the last reel on the late show. But the man in my life at those moments was never a suave, young Melvyn Douglas! That's probably all to the good, because deep down I know that I could never submerge my own ambition enough to concentrate on helping along the career of someone else—no matter how much I loved the guy. I'm very competitive and I'd be competing with him, too!"

Admire her candor or deplore her self-centeredness, but you have to admit that the world is probably a more peaceful place because she did not, at those "most despairing moments," give up and get married.

A friend I'll call Sylvia Steinfeld has gone back to work as a computer data analyst after four years of marriage, two children, and a nasty divorce. "Let's face it," she said, "I got married because I thought I was in love but I know for damn sure that I was bored with my job . . . tired of the same old routine and unable to break it. Well, I guess I didn't try too hard to break it because now that I'm back with more responsibilities, I've worked my way into a really interesting job that pays a lot better. Anyway, you could say that the routine before got to me and I started thinking that it would be fun to be home all day, to have a house in the country with grass and some flowers and a couple of kids and a dog or a cat. So I gave up my job. Quit and got married. Well, it was fun for a few weeks but then it got lonely as well as monotonous and I began to miss being around a lot of different people all day. Finally I started picking friendly fights with Chaz just to break the monotony and pretty soon the fights got so unfriendly that we agreed to see a couple of lawyers. I'll probably marry again some day, but you can be sure it won't be because I think marriage beats working."

Some women give up in business because they feel undervalued and underused. In San Francisco, during a radio talk show that included telephone conversations with listeners, a young woman told me about an unhappy experience she had just been through with a giant aircraft company. "I am a graduate engineer," she said, "and my grade average was one of the highest ever made at U.S.C. After a year with another aircraft company, I was recruited by Icarus [fictitious name] and thought I would get to do some real designing. The head of the department I went into said they were thrilled to have me there—pleased to have a woman on staff and anxious to see what ideas I could contribute.

"Well, they must not have wanted to see very much because all they gave me to do was junk. I got stupid assignments that any second-year engineering student could handle and wasn't really *designing* anything. They said be patient, I'd get some good stuff soon. But after six months of that garbage, I got disgusted and quit. I thought I could get another job, but so far I haven't. Mainly, I think, because I'm not getting a good reference from Icarus. The personnel department reports that I'm 'able—but have low job interest,' which is pretty deadly. So I'm still unemployed. I've got a

fairly good relationship going so I'll probably quit looking and get married."

A few minutes later an executive of Icarus phoned in.
He said he didn't know the engineer who had been
talking to me but was sorry to hear that she had quit so
quickly. "New engineers at our company are always
given routine assignments," he said. "It's a way of in-
doctrinating new employees. Even though they're graduate engineers with some experience, there's a lot that
has to be learned about our particular way of doing
things and they pick it up the first year with the company on these routine assignments—the things she described as junk and garbage. She should have stayed!"
At any rate, she should have talked with her boss or one
of the engineers who had been there longer than she
had and was doing the kind of work she wanted to
do.

Another reason why women give up their career ambitions stems from their attitude toward failure. They
don't handle it very well, reacting to their own fumbles
and bumbles on a very personal basis. As already mentioned, men have a self-protective way of dealing with
their own shortfalls and can dismiss major failure with
some such absolving comment as, "Well! *We* blew that
one, didn't we!" Women, under similar circumstances,
almost never look upon the lash-up as a group goof, but
as a very personal failure. To the female involved it's
strictly a matter of *mea culpa*—"*I* blew it. It's my fault,
I let it happen, maybe I'm not smart enough or strong
enough, maybe I shouldn't have this job, maybe I
shouldn't have any job at all."

This kind of wallowing in guilt and self-abnegation is

occasionally engaged in by men, but it happens mostly in Woody Allen movies, far removed from the jolly good fellows at the office. It is a peculiarly female trait, born of naïveté.

It is always healthy to look for the flaws in your own performance but it is sick, sick, sick to brood over what you did wrong. Maybe what you did wasn't wrong at all, and even if it was, you probably had help. The breakdown of a project or program is almost never the fault of any one person. The fatal finger may point at a particular action or inaction that was the immediate cause of the error, but there are other considerations, such as the circumstances of the moment, to say nothing of the overall emotional climate. At any rate, don't rush to cover yourself with guilt and blame. Don't duck, dodge, and double-talk—and above all, don't lie about it or try to blame somebody else. Just give yourself the celebrated "benefit of the doubt."

Nancy, who is a chemist in the product development department of a large pharmaceutical house in New Jersey, told me about a revolutionary new hair care product she had originated and developed for her company. It got an extraordinary reception from the marketing department and all the larger bosses, right up to the C.E.O.

"This was going to be our big superstar for 1980," she said. "We were putting most of the company's ad money behind it and expected it to grab off a sizable share of the market, easily increasing our sales 12 to 15 percent all by itself. This was a real winner! But I slipped up somewhere and we had to recall all of the first shipment and start over. Now the whole intro is

delayed and won't be ready for the most critical selling
quarter.

"To make it all worse, we had in the meantime cut
back other production to handle this—which means
that the company will operate in the red this year instead of flying ahead with my project. It also means
that I, of course, won't get my vice-presidency. I don't
even have the heart to remind them they promised me
one! The way I look at it, they're nice to keep me on
after I pulled a boner like that. How could I have done
anything so stupid"

Did you hear that, Dr. Freud? How could *she* have
done anything so stupid?

The real questions are these: how could she be so
innocent as to assume the entire blame herself? What
about all the other people involved? The ones who
actually ran the formula? Where were the quality control people? Where were the testers and supervisors,
bearers and beaters? Who were the geniuses who decided to stake so much of the company's future on one
product? Above all, why should the creator of a product
that will eventually make millions for the company be
denied a vice-presidency because somebody somewhere
down the line dumped the wrong gook into a vat and a
succession of others overlooked the error?

You can bet that these are the questions that would
be apoplectically shouted by a man in the same situation. You can also bet that he'd find a way to get his
promised vice-presidency, probably even bearing down
on his demands for it because he was so put upon by
the mishandling of his "baby."

Not Nancy. She will go right on groveling in the
ashes, heaping guilt on herself and convinced that it is

an act of charity for the company to let her stay there in any capacity. The day I talked to her she was thoroughly discouraged. "Frankly," she said, "I think it would be better for me to just stick to the routine around here. The head of my department was pleased when my product got such a big reception because it made the whole department look good—but when this happened, he let me know that it would be a lot safer for me to devote what talent I have to making his ideas work. He's got an idea for a four-seasons skin cream that he thinks will make women buy four times as much cream—four different products. I think it's for the birds! But I'm going to go back into the lab and put my head down and work quietly—on four-seasons skin cream. Like he said, it's safer. And any disappointment will be mainly his instead of mine." Too bad. She's a very gifted chemist with a lot of imagination and flair.

Nancy's reaction is not unusual. When women discover that there is as much fantasy, intrigue, and caprice at the office as there is in the average soap opera, they are baffled to the point of disbelief, and when they get caught up in the money-losing senselessness, they quit. They decide they're never going to understand it, never going to flourish or even survive on this bleak landscape, and hit for what is touted to be the sanctuary God made for them. Home Sweet Home. If circumstances—financial, romantic, or otherwise—won't permit this at the moment, they do the "next best" thing. They resign themselves to a small role, small status, small salary far below their accomplishment quotient.

Unhappily, most management men appear to be relieved when women settle down into routine back-up jobs. It is the dedicated female servants, breaking an intimate part of their anatomy to provide a strong and steady support system for male executives, who are genuinely cherished. The new "Lady Hot Shots" with advanced degrees, outfront ideas, and magnificent obsessions about their own careers are looked upon with growing dismay.

A young woman went to work last year for a Washington research firm, expecting to advance rapidly. She has a Ph.D. that she's understandably proud of and let it be known that she expected to be addressed as Doctor. This "didn't go down well" with the men at her level who did not have her impressive educational background but were seasoned professionals in the field. "They were gunning for me right from the start," she said. "Called me *Doctor* in a heavily sarcastic tone, and snickered when they said it. I just called them *Mister* in the same tone and snickered right back. That stopped them from calling me *Doctor* but they were thoroughly unpleasant to me. Never asked me to join their little luncheon groups, although they made a point of inviting others in my presence. I began to feel like a pariah, so I quit—which was what they hoped, I know, but I just couldn't take it. With my degree I can teach, but that's not what I want to do. What I really want is to become a vice-president of a prestigious firm like the one I was in, but I'm frankly disillusioned and discouraged. . . ."

Her discouragement is understandable but she shouldn't let the bad experience on her first job chase her out of a good field. It was only natural for her to resent the sarcasm of the men about her hard-earned Ph.D., but she should have recognized it as envy—and even anticipated it. She should not have made an issue of being addressed by an academic title and under no circumstances should have responded in kind to sarcasm about it. Having made the initial error, however, she should have been courteous and pleasant, giving the men no excuse to continue their treatment. As for feeling like a pariah at lunchtime, she could have avoided that by making lunch dates well in advance with people outside the firm instead of brooding alone over a sandwich at her desk.

Something similar started happening to a woman in Chicago who was getting a hard time from male associates about her doctorate. They called her Dr. Marvel and Wonder Woman, but she smiled and hung in there. "This seemed to make one of them even madder," she said, "and I was beginning to despair of the situation. It was really getting to me. Then one day *Newsweek* came out with an article headed 'THE PH.D. MEAT MARKET.' It was about the proliferation of doctorate degrees and the difficulty in providing enough teaching jobs for men and women spending five years earning them. One of my tormentors tore out the piece and posted it on the bulletin board with the words 'PH.D. MEAT MARKET' underlined in red. It so happens that the two founding partners of our firm are Ph.D.s and very proud of it. One of them got so blazing mad that he called in my tormentor and fired him, telling him that his lack of respect for academic credentials indicated poor potential."

Almost nobody welcomes criticism, and everybody

deals with it differently. I've seen men literally get fighting mad and come out swinging when their work was under fire. I've seen others go into a decline about it, and this, more often, is the female reaction. One woman quit a job in St. Louis that she really liked because her supervisor disagreed with a plan she wanted to put into action. "I spent days putting it together and organizing it all into a nice, tabulated report, giving all the pros and cons and working things out right down to the last detail. He called me in and chewed me out for wasting time. Said I should have given him a brief rundown first in outline form, but I wanted to be thorough and show him I had thought the whole thing through. When I quit, he was absolutely stunned. Said he had no idea I couldn't take constructive criticism."

This woman, of course, should have sounded out her supervisor on the matter before she put that kind of time and energy into it. If he had expressed doubt, she could have said, "Why don't I work up the details on this and let's go over them together." This would have given him an opportunity to let her know that he wasn't a bit interested in the project. At any rate, it would have set the stage for his introduction to the long report that had obviously been time-consuming. Since none of this had happened, she should have accepted the "chewing out" with equanimity, having learned that he had to be prepared in advance for a project. If you really like your job, you have to go along with the ideas and work habits of people who control your destiny.

Most of us know women who we think are as funny as Erma Bombeck, women who, in our opinion, should be tossing off delightful books and singing out one-liners on the lecture circuit as Bombeck does. We know others with shrewd, insightful minds and gifts of articulation who we're sure could compare with Barbara Walters! Why, we wonder, aren't they best-selling authors or million-dollar-a-year television stars?

What we don't know is how many rejection slips Bombeck collected before any of her witty prose got into print or how many weary hours she spent at the typewriter learning to make it all sound so easy. We forget, too, about the years Walters spent getting up in the middle of the night Monday through Friday to do the *Today* show and toiling to perfect her craft between on-camera appearances. There must have been numberless times when both of them wanted to walk away from the whole miserable effort, and either of them could have sold herself an acceptable excuse. But they hung in there and look what happened!

What happened no doubt has often been unfunny even to Bombeck and more dispiriting to Walters than getting up in the middle of the night to go to work. Is it worth it? Maybe it wouldn't be for you.

Maybe you're not out for that kind of money or celebrity. I know one altogether wonderful woman who says that all she wants to do is "sit in a corner and type faster than anybody else." She does. But it took determination to endure all those hours of practice with quick-brown-foxes-jumping-over-the-backs-of-lazy-sleeping-dogs. I also know a devastatingly clever woman in one of the burgeoning Sunbelt cities who originated a television show for the leading local station in 1971 and was overjoyed when it became an immediate success. After six months a new program manager at the station moved it to another time slot where it was overwhelmed by network competition. She did not originate another show or try to reactivate that one after the manager who made the change had been replaced. "My heart just isn't in it," she said. "I put everything I had into that show and when it got kicked around until it was killed dead, I had no interest in starting over with something else. What's the use? I don't think I could stand another disappointment like that!"

I know how she felt. Having had my share of rejections, I know how disheartening they can be. But I also know that the only way to take them is to try again— immediately. It's like getting back into an airplane as soon as possible after crashing. If you don't do it right away, you may never do it again.

A very great deal has been said about the virtue of "hanging in there"—but not enough. To date, the most colorful quote on the subject, if not the most penetrating, has come from Yogi Berra, baseball's ruling linguist since the demise of Casey Stengel. Yogi shrugged off his team's low standing in the 1978 pennant race by reminding the press, "It ain't over till it's over." It was mid-July and his crippled Yankees were stumbling miserably along in fifth place, where they seemed doomed to stay. In October they were Champions of the World, having staged one of the most incredible comebacks in the history of sports by hanging in there.

Although business is no baseball game, there are pennant races of one kind and another going on all the time, and you, of course, can't possibly be at the champagne cork popping if you've quit and gone home or given up the effort to get on one of the front-running teams.

Of course, it is tougher for a woman. But:

1. *Hang in there.* Dust off all the corny homilies you know about persistence, trial and error, perspiration vis-à-vis inspiration, and all that. If you have enough sophistication to tackle the world as a liberated woman, you should have enough to accommodate a little corn. So what's corny about power and fame and fortune? Look at the people who have them!

2. *Don't mistake a socially approved exit for an "easy out."* The ease can quickly go out—especially if the exit is a marriage you're jumping into mainly because you hate your job.

3. *Don't kid yourself that "anything would be better than this."* Things can always get worse and often do. If you're dissatisfied with things at work, talk it over with the person you report to—not your peers. A bit of bitching can be fun but it's amateurish and a waste of time.

4. *Give yourself (and the situation) a fair chance.* Things do change and it's no disgrace to change your own mind or attitude. It's foolhardy to go on fighting a battle that you don't have a chance to win, but be sure the chance has run out before you run out yourself. As Yogi said: "It ain't over till it's over!"

Chapter 5

The Party's Over

The down side of hanging in there is the built-in danger of staying in a place too long. It's hard to get out of a warm bed, even when you've come to dislike whoever is in there with you. A firmer mattress may be better for you now and you may realize that you prefer another kind of bedding. But there's a degree of comfort that's difficult to leave. Familiarity is often equated with safety and the tendency is to pull the security blanket up around your ears and linger. "Better a known monster than an unknown ogre." So it goes when you've settled into a job that's reasonably pleasant.

Added to your own feelings of comfort and safety are the reassurances of well-meant little compliments:

"You've got a good job—for a woman!"

"You're making good money—for a woman!"

Then one of these years you are shaken to realize

that the compliment has been lengthened. Suddenly you've got a good job and are making good money—for a woman your age! Of course, some of the very young women get the long form of the compliment, too, but usually as an admonition to be patient. The inclination to stick with a job stalemate is found most often in women over forty.

Six years ago, a woman who was head of food testing for a smallish manufacturer was offered a job in Seattle with a company twice as large at a big salary increase. She didn't take it because "Seattle seems so far away" and she wasn't sure she'd like it. "I felt very secure where I was," Libby said, "and I was afraid of being stuck out there in the Northwest and maybe not liking it a bit. I was interviewed for the job in New York and they offered to pay my way there to look the place over, but I decided it would be a waste of time and didn't go. The company was so big and the change just seemed too much!"

Last year Libby's company was merged with a much larger one, her department was folded into a comparable one in the bigger organization, and she is no longer head of anything—in a huge company! This makes her very unhappy. "I'm forty-one now and my prospects aren't as good as they were when I turned down the Seattle job at age thirty-five. The irony is that I visited the city a couple of summers ago on a tour of the Northwest and fell in love with the place! Also, I see the woman who did take the job at industry conventions—and she's deliriously happy. Obviously she's done very well."

Libby should at least have given Seattle a chance.

Since the company that wanted her was willing to pay
her travel expenses, she had nothing to lose but a weekend of her own. She knows now that she missed the
opportunity of a lifetime.

So did a friend of mine who turned down an extraordinary opportunity in Chicago. At the fateful time
she was involved with a man who was separated from
his wife. When my friend told him she was moving to
Chicago, he insisted that she stay in New York, declaring that he would get a divorce and marry her right
away. She didn't go to Chicago and he didn't get a
divorce. He went back to his wife and she went back to
the executive placement company that had recruited
her, but it was much too late.

My friend knows now that she should have gone to
Chicago. Jobs like that one are rare. "They come along
for people in my field about once in ten years," she says
woefully. "If things with Jim had worked out, we could
have worked out the job situation, too, because his
company also has a branch in Chicago. Even if this
weren't true, I shouldn't have made my career decisions
on the basis of his marital decisions when I knew they
were very uncertain."

Women who have abandoned their early ambitions
to plod along in nonpressure jobs may be surprised to
hear that they are not escaping that Old Devil, Stress,
and its much-discussed damage to body and mind.
"Look," I heard one young woman tell another, "you
can go on knocking yourself out at work if you want to
but I don't want to get into a rat race that's going to
give me a heart attack or some kind of breakdown. I
thought I wanted to set the world on fire. Everybody at

school expected me to! But it's just too tough for a woman. I'm settling into a nice, quiet job that's no sweat. Let somebody else get the ulcers. I'd rather give them than get them!"

The relation of stress to illness is under constant study and some of the investigations indicate that the young woman quoted above may be on the receiving end of the ulcers anyway, since there is indication that people stuck in jobs below their performance levels suffer the stress of frustration and boredom! The stress studies, as of now, are inconclusive. We know what drives monkeys crazy—and what makes rats kill each other—but we're not sure how this applies to people.

Sociologists and the press have commented at length on stress-related illnesses among women and the correlation of these to their new roles in the work force. Writing in a January 1980 issue of *The Wall Street Journal*, Joann S. Lublin commented on the rise in female alcoholism, heart disease, auto accidents, suicide, insomnia, depression, and crime, saying (among other things) this: "In the wake of the revolution in sex roles and gains in female employment, women are increasingly afflicted by a range of social and physical problems that used to be largely the domain of men. It is a phenomenon that some describe—in a much-disputed analysis—as 'the dark side of female emancipation.' "

Miss Lublin quoted sociology professor Alice Rossi of the University of Massachusetts as follows: "When you break the homebound nature of women's lives and get them into jobs, you're bound to get an elevation of their drinking, smoking and accident rates. It's the price of social change." Her even-handed story also cites assertions by leading feminists that the women's movement has improved the mental health of many women by giving them greater control over their lives and more self-respect.

The business world is full of ultra-effective one-job women who have been with the same company for ten to twenty years and longer. They are the very backbone of the department or, in smaller organizations, the whole business. They "know more about what goes on around here than the boss," they "know where all the bodies are buried," and most of them enjoy it enough to swallow the lump in their throats when they look at their paychecks. That is, they used to.

That was yesterday. Today's women have learned the value in moving on when the opportunities to move up where they work now have been exhausted or, for some reason, are nonexistent.

Twenty-seven-year-old Fran had gone to work for a carpet company in a midwestern city as secretary to the general manager. She had two years of previous experience and had attended junior college. Fran is a quick learner, likes detail, and knows how to keep her mouth shut about confidential matters. She was the ideal person to take over the company's medical and insurance records and gradually did, but she was unable to get the salary or status she deserved.

"I had been there six years," Fran said, "and my responsibilities had just about doubled. But I'm ashamed to tell you how little I was being paid. My boss was one of those male chauvinists who honestly believe that women were made to serve men and expected me to keep bringing him coffee, sharpening his pencils per-

sonally, and doing all the things for him that I was
hired to do in 1973—in spite of the fact that I was now
in complete charge of the medical and insurance records of over a hundred people.

"When small raises came through for me and I tried
to talk to him about a salary more in keeping with what
I was doing, he said he couldn't do anything about it
because my job title was 'secretary' and secretaries all
got the same increases. When I suggested that my job
title be changed, as it certainly should have been, he
said that was impossible. Being the general manager,
he, of course, had the authority to make the change,
but when I pointed this out, he flew into a rage and told
me how lucky I was to have a good job when there are
men my age who have families to support—as if that
had anything to do with it. I quit on the spot."

Fran got another job right away in the personnel department of a huge Milwaukee corporation and in one
year has become assistant manager at $14,500 a year.
She was getting less than $9,000 at the carpet company.
She was absolutely right to leave the company that refused to recognize her capability by adjusting both her
title and salary. Her requests were reasonable and she
was within her rights to discuss the matter with her
supervisor.

Anne Marie, who is twenty-nine, faced a similar situation in Portland, where she was the secretary of the
executive vice-president of a paper company. When he
discovered how bright and capable she was, he began
handing off more and more important work to her that
he had been handling himself. Each time she tried to
talk with him about a different job title with a larger
salary, he "gyrated like a helicopter out of control."

"He got very excited," Anne Marie said. "He'd start waving his arms and shouting that he had too much to do to sit around talking—and so did I. He'd say, 'Whatever it is that you've got on your mind will have to wait.' After I'd been there four years and he had been telling me periodically for two of them that whatever I had on my mind would have to wait, I wrote him a memo. It was short, unemotional, and to the point. I listed, numerically, in one sentence each, eight executive responsibilities I had relieved him of, giving the approximate date he had turned each of them over to me.

"My last paragraph read, 'This respectfully requests that my title be changed immediately to administrative assistant with a salary increase to $13,000 retroactive to January 1, 1979. If this cannot be arranged, please accept this as my resignation effective two weeks from this date.' "

How did he react?

"He didn't say anything at all to me for a whole day. Not even good morning or good night. I think he might have felt that the silent treatment would get to me and I would say something about the memo to him. The next day when I came back from lunch, my memo was back on my desk. He had underlined administrative assistant and $13,000 retroactive to January 1, scrawled 'Okay' in the margin, and signed it with his initials. The next day he dictated an announcement of my promotion to me and asked me to post it on the bulletin board. I still do his personal correspondence because he trusts me and I really don't mind doing it; in fact, I enjoy knowing all that's going on. The important thing to me is that I got my title and I got my raise!"

This was excellent strategy. Anne Marie's boss was evading the issue by staging an act—a big emotional scene that made discussion impossible. Since she couldn't talk to him, the only thing she could do, except resign, was write him a calm, brief memo stating the facts clearly and firmly. She also handled his silent treatment properly, not initiating any conversation with him until he replied to her memo.

When Anne Marie related this incident to me, we were having coffee with a friend of hers whom I'll call Sandy. Anne Marie turned to her and said, "You want to talk about what happened to you a few weeks later?"

"Sure," Sandy said. "Why not? I was going through just about the same thing where I worked—an insurance company. My boss had me doing everything for him. All of his work, except attending the big meetings with the top brass. When I approached him about moving up and getting more money, he was very courteous, agreed that I was doing work beyond my job description and salary level, and said he would 'take it up with them.' Never with whom. Just 'them.' Then I wouldn't hear another word about it until I brought it up again.

"When Anne Marie told me how her tactic had worked, I wrote him a three-page memo. I guess it was emotional but I got a lot of things off my chest. Among other things, I reminded him that I was thirty years old and not getting any younger, or any better looking doing so much of his work."

What happened?

"He fired me! Called me into his office right away and said he was sorry to know that I wasn't happy and was accepting my resignation with regret. He added that he appreciated my giving him two weeks' notice and knew he could count on me to train a replacement whom he'd asked Personnel to arrange for immediately."

"She was fired but it came out okay," Anne Marie said. "She got a great job before she could even give herself a little vacation. She started at the new place with more money than she had asked for where she was before and got a terrific raise in six months. She'll be a vice-president in another year and we'll all have to salute her! Why wasn't I lucky enough to be fired?"

Odds are that ten years ago none of these women would have moved and twenty years ago it probably wouldn't even have occurred to them to try. They most likely would have been grateful to be working at all. Time marches on!

An entirely different kind of experience was reported to me by a Boston printer who has watched the progress of a woman now in her late thirties, who started out working as a switchboard operator at a large printing plant in Boston. She had no training except what on-the-job instruction she received to familiarize her with the telephone system.

This is an unusually intelligent woman with a restless mind who soon grew bored with the switchboard routine. She went to night school, where she learned office skills that permitted her to apply for a job as secretary at the same company. She became the secretary of the man who managed the production department, quickly mastering a great deal of the detail involved in supplying printing.

Once again she set her sights higher. She wanted to

earn more money and felt that, to do this, she'd have to put her knowledge to work somewhere else. Although top management at her company appreciated her efforts, they were used to having her around at a lower level in both salary and position. When a giant textbook publisher offered her a job as a printing buyer at a huge salary increase, she panicked.

"I'm scared to death!" she told the friend who reported this to me. "What if I fail?"

"Don't be ridiculous," the friend replied. "You're a first-rate printing *supplier* now. You'll be a printing *buyer* at the other place. The exact same facts and figures are involved. You'll just be on the other end!"

The woman took the job. That was six years ago. Today her salary is dramatically higher—many times greater than her pay as the production manager's secretary. Now she has a new goal, a much higher one, of course. She is going to night school again and intends to get her master's degree in business administration. She feels that it is not unrealistic to shoot for a much larger job at that publishing company or another—maybe even a vice-presidency. Why not? Publishing is one of the areas where women are making tremendous gains and, according to knowledgeable executives in the field, so is the printing industry that services it.

Mature women with a solid base of experience and a lot of good years left are beginning to discover that other companies are eager to reward them for the expertise that is taken for granted where they are.

Mindy, who is forty-one, told me last September in Atlanta that she had "finally got up the courage to change jobs" and was happy as the clam that missed the clambake. Mindy had been a buyer in a Louisville store for eleven years. "It was the only place I ever worked," she said. "I started out there right after college, as a stockkeeper and worked my way up to assistant buyer in the budget suit department. Then I was made buyer for the California sportswear shop, and a couple of years later they added junior casuals and I was covering Seventh Avenue, too.

"When the man who was head buyer for all women's sportswear left, I got his job, but last year, when the sportswear merchandise manager retired, I didn't get that one. I had applied for it a year earlier when the M.M. told me his plans and the president said not to worry about it, just to keep plugging away and everything would be fine. I took that to mean I'd get the job, but I didn't. The president said they'd never had a woman merchandise manager and didn't think it would work out with the women buyers. I get along with all of them and they expected me to get the job. The new guy who did has made himself very unpopular with some new inventory systems that make everybody's job harder and actually caused a sales decrease. That cut the bonuses, mine included.

"When I got a chance at this new job as merchandise manager, I agonized over it for two weeks and then took the plunge. Am I glad! The store is smaller but the bonus percentages are better and that, on top of the salary increase I got, doubles my income."

What about the women buyers? Is it working out for them?

"Oh, yes! I had some problems with one of them at first but it's all right now."

And the men?

"Three men report to me here and, fortunately, they're a lot younger than I am. I say 'fortunately' because it's been my experience that the young ones are a lot more willing to accept women in positions of authority than most of the older ones. Our president is sixty, though, and he certainly has liberal ideas on the subject. The general merchandise manager is going to retire in two years and the president didn't say anything vague like 'don't worry' about getting that job. He said I'll definitely have it—period!"

Good for Mindy!

Why don't more of these underpaid, undervalued women move on to better things? Anne Hyde, president of Management Woman, an executive recruitment firm specializing in placement of women ($30,000-a-year minimum), says it can be summed up in one bleak, bad word: "Fear." Asked for more words, Hyde explains:

"Time and time again, I've seen very superior women walk away from spectacular opportunity when all systems were 'Go.' They've come to us brimming with confidence and determination, ready to move up the executive ladder to the positions their backgrounds have prepared them to command. We have matched their credentials up with corporations actively seeking gifted women for their executive staffs—only to have the whole thing come a cropper at the last minute!"

How so? With eyes shooting sparks, Hyde continues:

"We introduce a candidate to the corporate searchers. She passes muster with a battery of tough-minded executive men, makes a terrific impression, and they ask us to recruit her—perhaps at a salary twice what she's getting and more. At the moment of truth, she panics. Panics! The confidence and determination collapse. She says she's sorry but she's afraid she wouldn't be right for the job. The key word is afraid—and the fear is infuriating because I know and the executive men know that she could do the job brilliantly. I could *swear!*"

Yes, Anne! Damn that fear. This is something else women have that men don't—or if men do have it, not many let it hold them back. Self-doubt comes between many a woman and the fulfillment of her potential. Men are willing to go charging into situations that aren't exactly right for them because they have confidence enough to give it a shot when it represents progress.

A woman I know who is head of a department at a major insurance company accepted a position with a New Jersey corporation a few months ago at a salary increase of 63 percent! Her old employers were desolate. They would not match the salary but offered her a 20 percent raise and dramatized the family feeling she would be leaving behind, the warm camaraderie, the security she enjoyed. First one executive and then another gave her the company pep talk, urging her to stay. At the last minute she capitulated. She called the New Jersey people and told them she was sorry but she would not be joining them after all.

I talked to her last week and asked if she's sorry. "In a way, yes," she said. "I know I should be earning that much money, but when the chips were down, I felt better about staying where I am." In a warm bed! She should put on her marching clothes and take advantage of the opportunities that come her way, while they're still coming.

Kate Rand Lloyd, now editor-in-chief of *Working Woman*, is a woman who had the courage to strike out in a new direction after thirty years with one organization. Although she had progressed through a series of important editorial positions, she had not held the top slot on any of the magazines where she had functioned as a steadily charging spark plug. She looks back on her pre-*Working Woman* career like this: "I think I remained with one organization all those years because it was comfortable and secure, and in those years comfort and security meant more to me than challenge. Now that my children are grown up, I like the stimulation of going places, professionally, where nobody's been before. Like many women who are moving up, we have no role models. Each issue represents a step onto new ground. And I find that exhilarating! Now I wonder how I ever lived without this kind of growth experience."

Marian Tripp was a one-company woman for twenty years before she started her own public relations firm in New York and Chicago. Marian says, "The nesting instinct is strong in women. Legendarily so, and at the same time very real. Men don't build nests because women build nests for them. Nest builders aren't big risk takers for the simple reason that they couldn't stand to see any of their carefully placed twigs fall out of the tree!

"Sometimes I think about all the risks I took when I went into business for myself in 1976 and wonder where I got the courage. I had two sons in college and no nest egg to fall back on."

Has she ever been sorry?

"Certainly. A few times—for a few minutes. But never for long. I love being in a situation where I can make *all* the major decisions myself. Mainly who my company will and will not work for. That, to me, is the world's greatest luxury."

Everything inside me stands up and cheers for the women who have the courage to make changes that advance their careers and provide opportunities for new growth and development. But for every one of these, there are dozens of gifted women who work hard and are abundantly productive—for somebody else. They drag out their careers in a mire of boredom, doing the same old things at the same old places when they have everything it takes to succeed at challenging jobs and lead exciting, doubly productive lives.

Most large companies and an increasing number of small ones are operated on the "carrot principle." In an effort to keep people in place, to discourage them from looking around for greener pastures, concerned employers dangle the brightest benefit package (or carrot) they can. The package is, of course, made up of an appealing cluster of various elements, such as stock options, low-interest mortgages, free or low-cost medical plans and insurance, child education, adult education, retirement programs, free or low-rent vacation facilities, company cars, use of corporate airplanes, and expense allowances.

Most of these benefits are based on good intentions, since they, in some ways, "save us from ourselves," representing built-in future planning. Human nature being what it is, people of both sexes tend to live for the moment without much brooding about the future. We bandy clichés about: you're only young once; eat, drink and be merry for tomorrow we may die; tomorrow may never come and what difference will it make anyway a hundred years from today? The benefit packages permit practice of these devil-may-care philosophies with a clear conscience.

Inasmuch as their escalation and eventual payoff are, quite naturally, based on length of service, their effect is to keep some employees around to their own (or the company's) detriment. Key executives in some of America's largest, most powerful corporations privately admit that the benefits in many instances "underwrite mediocrity." They can also underwrite self-limitation. These packages are important extras that should be examined carefully when you are considering a job offer, but they should not control your life. Basing your career on security only clamps restraints on your mobility and, therefore, limits opportunity to develop your own potential and enjoy your own unique talents.

Betsey has been the chief bookkeeper for a large Baltimore department store for seven years. She has been employed there all her working life—a total of sixteen years—and has accrued substantial benefits. She is, of course, "vested" and will receive an agreeable pension if she stays until she's sixty-five. Last year Betsey was offered the position of controller at another company at a large increase, but she turned it down. "I thought I'd lose out on too many nice benefits," she said. "They didn't look as good at the other place. But I might have made a mistake."

Betsey did make a mistake. Because she is a bookkeeper, she understands figures but she doesn't understand legalese and that's the language benefit packages are written in. She should have reviewed the offer with an attorney to make a valid comparison. Betsey has discovered that the pension she is counting on is actually ninety-three dollars a month less than she thought —and besides, inflation has diminished its importance even more.

Women have been known to remain in situations that were unhappy or unproductive for them because they're afraid that a lot of job changes will "look funny" on a résumé. They won't if you had a good reason to make them, and changing for the sake of better opportunity is something management understands. Besides, you don't have to tell the whole fascinating story of your life on a résumé or include every minute detail of your employment record. It's never smart to lie on a résumé, but it is good business to focus on the facts that relate importantly to the job you're applying for. Skip the extraneous stuff and concentrate on the relevant specifics. It saves everybody's time.

How is a woman to know when to hang in there and when to move on? Naturally, the options differ with age, family situation, and goals, but here are some general guidelines:

> 1. *If you haven't had a raise or praise in a year and a half* or if your raise is a routine one passed along without comment, it's about time to move.
>
> 2. *If your area of authority has been steadily eroded* or the people who should respond to your requests don't pay any attention to them, it's about time.
>
> 3. *If the above things have happened and you*

still want to stay there yet feel effectively cut off from optimum performance, ask for an appointment with someone who can change things—the person you report to or, if you've done that and it hasn't worked, someone higher in the pecking order. If the appointment doesn't materialize or doesn't bring about an open discussion with satisfying results, it's about time.

4. *Remember that company benefits alone are not enough.* Weigh the pension and whatever else you're going to get against your potential someplace else—carefully, with an attorney. There is always choice. You may think you have to stay there but there are options. Examine them with an open mind and a spirit of adventure. I enjoy remembering the comment of a friend in Jackson, Mississippi, Tee Lavelle, when she left a place she disliked intensely: "I was looking for a job when I got this one." Tee didn't particularly like job hunting but she understood that the world is full of opportunities and we, in turn, are full of natural resources. Don't sweat out a mismatch for the sake of a pension. You should have a more challenging goal than retirement, anyway. Living is now—the only time you are ever sure to have.

Chapter 6

A Matter of Style

One of management's reigning "buzz" words is style.

What's a buzz word? Buzz, itself, is one of them, a word from the daily jargon familiar to business and industry. Dozens of them crop up, some vanishing in a matter of weeks, others entrenching themselves permanently in the language of the trade. Although there are a few people, mostly language snobs and purists, who won't go along with any cliché for any reason, it's a good idea to learn the vocabulary of your business and an even better idea to use it. The buzz words can make people think you know what you're talking about even when you don't, which is one reason why they exist. Another more admirable reason is that they are a kind of spoken and written shorthand and, in this context, language is a part of Style.

Management Style is whatever the chief executive

officer says it is. As more and more women reach the executive level that brings them into contact with the C.E.O., it is important to understand the power of his office and the prerogatives he may exercise. He is answerable only to the board of directors, who usually go along with his wishes, leaving him free to do pretty much as he pleases. His style is Management Style, the manner in which the company's business is conducted.

Like the lady with the louse on her bonnet in the famous Robert Burns poem, the C.E.O. may have delusions about his own persona that have little or nothing to do with the reality of the matter. His actual behavior may differ dramatically from the way he wants it to appear or may earnestly believe it to be, but never mind. If you want to get ahead and stay there, you have to realize that part of your job is to reinforce his self-image while doing the best job you can. If, occasionally, these two things seem incompatible, don't give yourself ulcers about it and by all means don't comment on it. The C.E.O.'s ego is a dynamic force in the company's operations, and in most companies there is room to accommodate his personal foibles within the bounds of good business. At any rate, pleasing him with your own behavior, as well as with what goes on in your department, is a living, breathing factor in your progress.

The most successful "success book" in this century is *How to Succeed in Business Without Really Trying*, a wicked satire on the American corporation written by an ad man named Shepherd Mead and published in 1952. It was first a best-seller, then a long-running Broadway show, and finally a smash-hit movie that still attracts huge audiences for its periodic reruns. Over-blown though it is, Mead's comedy is classic because it caricatures business archetypes everybody knows, act-ing out work situations that everybody has either lived through personally or heard about many times from others. It is slapstick based on the nucleus of truth that marks all enduring comedy.

In *How to Succeed in Business Without Really Try-ing*, Finch, the young-man-in-a-hurry, finds out all that he can about the company's chief executive officer—his personal interests, tastes, and habits, the elements that add up to Style. He panders to these shamelessly and confidently, being the kind of young man who can gaze into his own eyes in the washroom mirror and sing "I Believe in You," one of the most delightful love songs ever written.

Of course, the joke within the joke of all this is that Finch *was* really trying, since his devious methods of "making it" require harder work than the accepted forms of diligence. Scheming does require greater effort than planning and, while there will never be any lasting substitutes for knowledge and for skill in applying it, the machinations that develop as temporary substitutes are familiar to us all.

Dastardly though Finch's tactics were, he *was* right in cultivating interest in the activities dear to the heart of his boss. If tennis is Mr. Big's game, you don't have to bring in a case of tennis elbow or even be a weekend player, but you should at least know who's winning and losing the big matches. You should also know which are his "favorite charities" and be responsive to any indica-tion that he'd like you to pitch in and help with one of them. Community leadership is, as it ought to be, a part of his Style.

A friend of mine who knows her way around on the corporate terrain points out that the C.E.O. is often joined in setting the company Style by his wife. In *How to Succeed in Business Without Really Trying*, Finch's boss had a secret lech for bubble-headed ingenues, which occasionally does happen in real corporate life— but not often. Generally speaking, the C.E.O. is a man whose drives have all been channeled into business and whose private life is shared only by people who in some way aid and bolster him in his work. If his wife becomes a personal handicap (an alcoholic, an indiscreet "playgirl," a blabbermouth), he divorces her or effectively excludes her from most of his life, keeping her well out of sight. Otherwise, she's practically part of the corporate logo. She may even turn up as company pitchwoman, doing commercials on local television.

Your C.E.O.'s wife may not be the most inspiring woman in the world, but if she has kept her place at his side, you can bet that she is one of the most influential people in yours. She may be a nondescript hausfrau, a gifted sculptor, a scintillating socialite, a revered community leader, or an absolutely fabuloso-cracking-nut . . . if she knows you, it's important for her to approve of you, regardless of what you may think of her.

One hapless woman I know who was at the brink of being employed by a major corporation struck out miserably with the wife of the C.E.O. when she lunched with the two of them, knowing that she was being subjected to another woman's evaluation. "I admit it," Francesca said, "I resented being 'cased' by someone who has never worked a day in her life and has absolutely no background for judging my qualifications. I suppose my resentment showed because I was not offered the position after all. It paid $80,000 a year to start, which would have been a sizable increase for me and, of course, I'd enjoy having it! But if I pleased the C.E.O. *and* that wife of his, I'm sure I'd earn every penny of it."

So am I. Eighty thousand dollars a year is a lot of money and the people who pay it expect every penny of it to be earned unless they are merely employing a corporate symbol. They also want to be as sure as they can be about the people they hire, and since that company had not previously employed a woman at such a lofty level, the C.E.O. wanted a "woman's opinion." The woman whose opinion he respects most is his wife's, and when she reacted badly to Francesca, that was all for Francesca.

I mentioned this incident to a group of women who instantly went into a rage over the "unfairness and stupidity of corporate thinking." Unfair or stupid, brilliant or just, the thinking behind corporate policy and practice must be coped with by people of either sex who want to be involved with the corporation. It is not at all rare for high-level executives to ask for—and accept!—the opinion of people who may seem extremely inappropriate but who, for some reason, enjoy the confidence of the executives who turn to them. It is certainly within the realm of reason for a man to trust his wife's judgment—particularly when he's asked her for it. Francesca should have behaved at the luncheon as she would have on any social occasion that is underpinned with business. She should have been gracious with a degree of caution thrown in, taking as many cues as possible from Mme. C.E.O. Instead, Francesca was aloof and unresponsive. When her hostess ordered white wine, Francesca didn't follow suit. She took pleasure in asserting her executive independence by ordering vodka on the rocks and quickly signaled the waiter to bring her another. She also skipped dessert, ordering cognac instead and holding forth about high calories while her slightly overweight hostess self-consciously worked on chocolate mousse. No wonder Francesca didn't get the job.

Adapting your own style to management's may be a breezy thing for you, thoroughly in keeping with your own tastes and preferences. If so, you're lucky. But getting along means going along with it whether you like it or not. A sense of humor helps.

The Style currently most favored is "Participative Management," which is nothing more than buzz terminology for the old, familiar Team Management, also known at one time and another as Group Think and Brainstorming. A male friend of mine, a major executive with a huge conglomerate, explains it like this:

"In Participative Management 'input' is solicited from all concerned. Everyone contributes ideas and positive or negative opinions about whatever program or project is under consideration. The C.E.O. then analyzes and distills all the opinions and announces a course of action—which is usually what he was planning to do anyway before all the memos were exchanged and all the meetings took place. All of which is just the long way of telling you the only participation that counts in Participative Management is the C.E.O.'s. What he usually has going is a simple corporate dictatorship."

What's the point in wasting everybody's time on the "input"?

He grinned. "That," he said, "is a very big thing in what is called Management by Motivation. You know how that goes: you give people a warm, happy sense of contributing to big decisions by asking for their ideas and opinions. The memos and meetings are like the suggestion box. They give people a chance to air their opinions and feel like they're making a difference."

Isn't that cynical?

"Yes," he admits. "And you know I'm exaggerating. But not much. If anybody at our company does have a hot idea, the best way to get it put into action is to give it to the top man quietly and *obliquely* so that he can take it up as his own!"

Of course, there are Styles within Styles and these must be coped with, too. Your supervisor has one, and if it doesn't blend into the Big Picture, there's hell to pay—for you, too, as well as the supervisor. Sooner or later the nonblender fades away. Meanwhile, you can't afford to offend the person who can get you fired or promoted.

A young woman in Philadelphia complained to me six months ago about her immediate superior at a manufacturing company. He was the man who headed a key department—largely, said she, because he was a relative of the president (like the nephew in the fictional company where Finch worked).

"I don't know how he gets away with it," she said,

"even with his family connections. He's a lazy slob who doesn't do anything but sit at his desk playing with figures all day. He loves what he calls 'the numbers' while the Big Boss, who enjoys being, by his own definition, 'a people person,' says over and over that the bottom line is made by people, not by the numbers themselves.

"Jeff (my supervisor) couldn't care less about people. He's imperious and condescending, treats everybody like dirt, and never asks anybody what they think about anything since he believes his opinion is the only one that counts. Our C.E.O. (Jeff's uncle) is all over the place and so are the rest of the men in the top echelon, listening to ideas and talking things over one on one. Anyway, I have to do all the work while Jeff takes all the credit for anything good that happens and chides me constantly about paying more attention to the numbers. 'You've got to know your numbers,' he says. . . ."

The other day, I saw her again and she happily told me that Jeff is out of her life and she now heads the department herself! What happened? "Well, they didn't fire him," she said. "He's still a member of the family so they've created a job for him in the accounting department. He can play with numbers there to his heart's content and it keeps him out of the way. He was a bottleneck before, and his uncle finally realized he wasn't going to change his way of doing things."

This smart young woman employed excellent strategy. She managed to get along with Jeff by making a big thing of the figures in his presence and by making the necessary contacts with other people (whom he found irritating) as unobtrusively as possible. Now that she's head of the department, she makes those contacts as noticeable to the C.E.O. as she can. He's a "people person" and it pleases him.

As a woman, your chances of becoming a C.E.O. at a major corporation remain dim. It has been pointed out that the "Fortune 500" companies offer only 500 opportunities for somebody to become C.E.O. and, at this writing, no one in this enchanted circle is female. A few women have made it to the rarefied top spot in an important company. And if you're ambitious enough to have an eye on such a spot, regardless of the odds, good for you! No matter where you are now, keep the other eye out for Management Style and start developing your own Style within the Style.

This is always difficult for women. First of all, there are few high-level female executives to emulate, and if you pattern yourself after the male ones, somebody is going to scream bitch or butch. They're likely to scream something unpleasant anyway, since getting ahead seldom wins popularity for either sex—especially with the people you get ahead of—and most especially when your gender is female. Being the boss does not diminish enjoyment of affection and admiration in a woman, just as it does not diminish the desire for it felt by almost any man. He looks at himself while shaving and she looks at herself while putting on makeup with the same basic emotions. They are both ego-centered, sensitive, stubborn, anxious, suspicious, gifted, hardworking, dedicated, and driven or they wouldn't be where they are. The big difference is that she is still a great deal more vulnerable than he is—and knows it!

Where women are concerned, Style is often confused with clothes or, at best, concentrated on them—under-

standably, because businesses are sensitive to appearances and people are part of the company decor. In
many industries women have slavishly followed the
dress-for-success "rule books," to the delight of old-line
clothing establishments. New York's Brooks Brothers,
for instance, is said to be enjoying a windfall "run" on
the neatly cut little man-tailored suit, worn with a silk
shirt, string tie, and medium-heeled pumps.

Management Style, however, is a great deal more
than clothes. It is the whole man and the whole woman
at work. Like it or not, appearances *are* a subject for
more concern to women, since men do feel free to be
critical of female faces and shapes, regardless of what
might have happened to their own.

Annharriet Buck, director of The Golden Door, the
world-famous California health spa (and "please don't
call it a 'fat farm'") says this: "The median age of our
clientele here is getting younger and we are attracting
enthusiastic groups of businesswomen as well as so-
cialites and celebrities from the entertainment world.
Career women are increasingly interested in physical
fitness and they tell us they prefer taking their vaca-
tions here where they can follow a controlled program
of diet, exercise, rest, and all-round physical rehabilita-
tion. Better, they say, than a vacation that leaves them
overstuffed with food, logged with drink—and exhausted!"

Margaret Adams, *Good Housekeeping*'s senior editor
for national affairs, says her observation is that "it's not
so much a matter of looking chic as looking well, able,
'with it.' It's not necessary to be a great beauty or a
perfect thirty-six or younger than springtime, but it *is*

important to look like the woman who gets the job
done!" Adams's *Good Housekeeping* job is just one of
the many she's constantly getting done.

Management Style also requires a certain amount of
playacting, which is engaged in even by people who
profess to abhor any hint of pretense, and some of the
people who abhor it loudest practice it all the time.

To be a good manager it is necessary, first of all, to
get your point across in a way that is understood and
remembered. If nobody knows what you're talking
about or remembers what you said, you might as well
have kept your mouth shut. Don't be afraid to dramatize a matter that makes your point solidly and gets it
remembered.

The office manager for a large company where the
telephone bill is astronomical is a woman I know. She
sent around half a dozen memos imploring employees
to cut out unnecessary calls and keep all calls within
the three-minute limit whenever possible. She held
meetings and "ranted" about it. The telephone bill remained astronomical. Then one day she called a meeting and asked everybody present to lend her all the
money they had with them. She added forty-seven dollars from her own purse, then counted out two hundred
from the collection, put her wastebasket on top of a
desk, dumped the money into it, and set it afire. "That's
how much money we're throwing away every week on
unnecessary phone calls!" she said. Then she put out
the fire before the flames had consumed all the green-
backs. There was a great deal of merriment about burning up the money completely to make the point even
stronger, but everybody remembered the demonstration and the phone bill went down.

Histrionics can, of course, get out of hand, as they did with a woman who was determined to make a big splash on Seventh Avenue. She spent three months on the Italian Riviera sunbathing, then came to New York with a phony Italian accent and a phony Italian name —say, Scarletti. She got two jobs on the basis of the act she was staging, but because she had never learned her craft, she was bounced out of each job after less than a season. "Scarletti" should have spent her time studying fashion designing and, perhaps, the Italian language, instead of lying in the sun. Seventh Avenue is notoriously susceptible to personal promotion, but unless the person running the promotion makes money for the company, she or he is told good-bye any Friday without previous discussion.

The herd instinct is one of the strongest in nature and all of us take comfort in following it. There is security in doing "what everybody else is doing," which accounts for some rather amazing fads in words, music, places, dances, food, entertainment, and even people. Most of them are harmless, some of them healthy, and a few downright dangerous. Over and over we are told to be ourselves, but insecurity being what it is, few people ever believe there could be much percentage in that. It seems safer to copy whatever has succeeded for somebody else. Yet the names that go up in lights on Broadway or in business are unfailingly those associated with a clear identity, and the ones that stay there are said to be those of people who are "inimitable." They are so completely themselves that imitation is virtually impossible and can be accomplished only through caricaturing—which sets the caricaturist down as merely an imitator.

At the lower levels of business conformity is a "must," but that doesn't mean drowning your own identity. There are companies known to favor people of a certain background—regional, educational, religious, ethnic— and if you're from another part of the country, went to another school, belong to a different church, or follow other customs, you may be tempted to masquerade a bit in order to get ahead. Don't. Some people manage to do this for a long time, but sooner or later the facts surface or the real you comes thundering (or shining) through.

Billie Sue from Nowhere, Tennessee, went to work for a small Knoxville radio station as a newscaster, right out of state university. She worked her way up the East Coast to larger and larger stations in larger and larger cities, then seemed to "bog down." She missed a job in Boston and thought it was because the manager "heard the South in my mouth, after I told him I'm from Tennessee." Thereafter she pretended to be from New York and made a big thing of it.

Sylvia is Jewish but went to work for a WASP company. She determined to conceal her religious and ethnic background and made a point of doing so, showing up for work on the Jewish holidays and occasionally making an anti-Semitic remark.

Both women were unhappy and didn't do well at their jobs. Guarding their real identity was a constant drain of time and energy. When Sylvia got tired of it and announced that she's Jewish, her life became "100 percent nicer" and she felt marvelous about herself. "Guess what?" she laughed. "The C.E.O.'s wife is Jewish; they've invited me to their home several times and

I've had a couple of nice promotions." Billie Sue didn't get up the courage to say she's from Tennessee until a Birmingham company bought the station where she was posing as a New Yorker, but she's vastly relieved that the masquerade is over and plans never to try it again. Granted, neither woman should have involved herself in such a small-minded effort, but insecurity breeds a lot of inanity.

What if the wife of Sylvia's C.E.O. had not been Jewish? And what if Billie Sue's station had not been bought by a Southern company? Who knows? At any rate, maintaining a pose that denies your origin adds needlessly to the demands of a job. It's a lot more fun to be yourself, to cultivate whatever you've got that's different instead of hiding it—unless it's something that's altogether socially unacceptable. Barbara Walters's trouble with pronouncing the letter "R" did not keep her from becoming the television superstar she is, and the impediment that brings it across as "wah" has become a mark of identification.

Every major company has a logo (short for logotype)—a special design used to display the company name, often accompanied by a symbol that is meant to indicate what the company makes, does, or is. Many an executive woman strives to acquire a personal logo with varying degrees of success.

One of the early "power books" relates the adventures of an executive woman who was said to have appropriated blue as her very own personal color. She wore no other, inspired her female employees to wear the same shade, thus identifying themselves as her troops, and ordered its exclusive use in the decor of her department—right down to such utilitarian equipment as filing cabinets. Apocryphal or not, the story should not tempt other executive women to take a mono-chromatic approach to their jobs. This is the kind of extraneous dedication to picayune detail that gets women branded "lightweight" and is conducive to cheap-shot ridicule.

All of us have known women who have swooped down on pink, yellow, green, red, turquoise, or even puce, laying claim to the color as theirs and declaring that it must be used on everything concerning them and nowhere else, regardless of appropriateness or anything else. Once I worked with a woman who drove everybody crazy wearing a Charles Addams-ish lavender until she heard it described by the office wit as "Mrs. Menopause's Purple." That did it! The joker got fired because the lavender lover was the boss. But she immediately got into a rainbow of other colors, mercifully before the lavender carpet she had requisitioned for the area had been dyed to order.

The personal logos I've seen that work are small marks of identification, usually jewelry, such as the turquoise worn by Ruth Oviatt, who is marketing and sales director of the trade magazine called *American School Food Service Journal.*

Speaking of office wits, if you have an overactive sense of humor, it's better to keep it on hold in most business situations. A well-timed "funny" can defuse a tense moment but an ill-timed one can cause an explosion that blows you right out of the running, even though you don't hear any sound at the time except laughter. Unless you know everyone present well enough to anticipate their response to levity, enjoy your little joke privately or share it with a friend later.

In Charleston there is a delightfully comic woman, locally famous for her howlingly funny one-liners. She let one of them fly at a conference she was invited to by a new boss who was going over budget figures with a worried client. The silence was deafening—until the client left. Then the boss howled, all right—but with rage. "We were discussing money," he reminded her woodenly, "and for your information, there is nothing funny about money!"

Annie is even quicker with the quips. Everyone thought she was a natural for the San Diego firm where she went to work last year because the man who owns it is a stand-up comic who emcees all the big programs at her industry's national conventions. He tosses off witty remarks around the office all day and Annie had a marvelous time topping them. She consistently got louder, longer laughs than he did—while she was there. But Annie doesn't work there anymore.

Annie was fired because "she just didn't seem to understand that business is, deep down, really serious," and Jill went elsewhere when she decided that her boss would never quite trust her discretion with clients. Both of them now realize the error in their witty ways. The ability to see humor in dark corners is priceless and the gift for making other people laugh can add an enviable element to Management Style. But knowing when *not* to make a funny is the sense in "sense of humor." The best policy is: when in doubt, DON'T!

Management Style—any company's, any executive's —may be indefinable. I asked a number of people I admire to give the definition a try and they gave me a lot to think about. Their replies make up an interesting mix of ideas and I'd say that anybody who manages to keep the whole mix together certainly has Style. Here's what their opinions boiled down to:

Style is doing what you said you were going to do when you said you were going to do it.

Style is getting where you're supposed to be, no matter what's coming down: rain, hail, sleet, snow, or owl feathers from Arkansas on the tail of a tornado.

Style is accepting defeat gracefully but with a quiet resolution that things will be different next time. (Show me a happy loser and I'll show you someone who's about to lose again.)

Style is passing up a chance to get even with an associate who's done you nothing but dirt. Revenge is sweet only for a moment; the consequences can last a lifetime.

Style is keeping control—of yourself first! You can't hope to control anything else if you've lost your grip on yourself.

Style is smiling at someone whose face you'd like to break if the smile helps you do your job. It's also chewing out someone you cherish for the same reason.

Style is listening when you'd rather be talking, working when you'd prefer to be playing, and starting over when you're worn out with the whole thing and don't really have the heart to.

Developing a style of your own that blends with any other is difficult, and if you discover that this is not how you want to do things, be prepared to move on—to another job, another company, or even a business of your own.

Getting ahead means, in two words, getting ahead. That, in turn, means breaking out of the crowd. Being different. Being, as the Irish say, yourself alone.

So how can a woman cope with all this? It's a situation delicate as dandelion fluff but this can help:

1. *Develop a style of your own but be sure it blends with overall Management Style at your company.* That means if the C.E.O. is machine-gun paced, give him fast, concise answers—bare facts, briefly stated. If he enjoys ruminating over details, use the long form with lots of whereases and on the other hands.

2. *Conduct your contacts with the C.E.O.—and his wife—on an individual basis.* Any foregone conclusions you might have formed about them from corridor rumors could be wrong and probably are. Be alert and pay close attention to whatever they say to you and proceed accordingly. You can be courteous and considerate without being syco-phantish. They may be rich and famous (and thoroughly spoiled by it!), but they're also human, responsive to small gestures. It won't hurt you to make them.

3. *Don't assume that the Finch formula for suc-ceeding in business without really trying can work offstage.* Finch's style was fun and we all know

people who get away with some of it, but the idea
that it can get you anywhere except out is pure
fiction. You've got to know the territory, which involves familiarity with Finch's tricks, but you've
also got to know your job and every job that
touches it.

4. *Be yourself.* While it is important not to
clash with corporate Style, there is always room
for you to cultivate your own individuality, and
the things about you that are different are the
things that make you remembered. How can they
promote you if you don't even cross their minds?

It Doesn't
Grow on Trees

In the none-too-bygone past, men told their income and
women told their age only to lie about it. Our country
clubs and restaurants have rung with male boasts of
salaries, expense accounts, and killings in the market,
while women in the same settings have fallen warily
silent when conversation turned to subjects apt to
"date" anybody who wandered into the trap of Remembering When.

In the interesting passage that has occurred, men
show a marked penchant for understating their age and
women for overstating their earnings. Emotionally
healthy or not, the sexes are almost equally concerned
now about age and personal income. The youth wor-
ship in business has sent graying male executives flying
into the Color Back bottle with all the anxiety of a
politician in an election year, and the career cult among
women has touched off some exaggeration in their

ranks about salaries. Naturally women handle the age matter more smoothly and the men are more clever about the money. In both cases it's a matter of background and experience.

Most women, however, remain strangely reluctant to discuss their own income with the people who pay them. One woman told me she would much rather talk to a job interviewer or boss about sex than money—and I believe her. "No fooling," she said, "I'd rather spill all the lurid details of my hottest involvement than sit there haggling like a fishwife about how much!"

She is not alone. Women loaded with worldly savvy flounder into paroxysms of embarrassment when discussing a price for their services. There is a lingering suspicion in the minds of both sexes that money is male and for women to be concerned with the stuff is unbecoming and "unfeminine," much the same as if they went sailing blithely into the men's room.

Traditionally the money women have had is whatever sums men have had the generosity to give them while living, or the forethought to leave them at death. Women are, therefore, at a disadvantage in negotiating salary or fees—especially so since the second party is apt to be male.

Businesswomen of all ages admit that the idea of money's maleness comes thundering through anytime they feel constrained to talk about it to men. "I don't know what gets into me," a woman named Marge told me in San Francisco. "There is no doubt in my mind that I'm worth $5,000 a year more than I'm getting. But I just sat there like a dummy last June when my boss went through his performance review of my work with me and showed me he'd given me an excellent rating on everything . . . then told me I was getting a $750-a-year raise. When I didn't say anything, he said, 'Well, isn't that great?' And I said, 'Oh, yes. Sure! Thank you very much. I guess I *had* hoped for a little more . . .' He just beamed and said 'Well, now, Marge, you just keep hoping and keep up the good work and I'll do my best for you. You know I'll take care of you.' Isn't that ridiculous?"

It is ridiculous indeed that a woman who can turn in such an excellent job performance for her company can't turn in a better one for herself when she talks about compensation for it. I asked a young man her age (twenty-eight) in the same city what he would have done under those circumstances and this was his reply:

"What do you mean what would I have done? I did it! Practically the same thing happened to me, except my company doesn't show us job reviews. The supervisor does tell us about them, though, and mine told me everything was fine except attendance—that I'd been absent two days more than allowed, but I was getting a $1,000 raise anyway. I thanked him but told him I had been working very hard with the expectation of a much bigger increase. Also that my attendance record was caused by the prolonged illness and death of my father, which required me to make a lot of trips to Pasadena. But I reminded him that I had more than made up for those days by working nights. I wasn't argumentative. Just stated facts, told him I had expected at least $3,000 more and was sure the record showed I had earned it. He said he'd 'take it up with them' and I said, 'Thank you! I'll check with you again on Friday of next week.' I did. I didn't get $3,000 but did get $2,000 and the promise of another increase in six months!"

This contrast in attitudes helps to perpetuate the notion that women don't understand money and can't handle figures. ("They don't know their numbers.") Actually, a great many women have computers between the ears but have been intimidated by their legendary lack of aptitude in the area. In some cases it is not a matter of intimidation. For reasons of her own, the woman in the scenario elects to conceal a computerized mind with her own petticoats.

In 1979 Mary Kay, the Texas cosmetics tycoon, told the press that her son manages the financial side of her corporation because "women don't know anything about money." The redoubtable Ms. Kay said this with a straight face, in spite of the fact that she has amassed a sizable fortune, aided mainly by an army of well-heeled women who have built up profitable little businesses of their own selling her cosmetics door to door. Kay's statement possibly reinforces her own view of femininity, which is reflected by her promotional program: she awards mink coats, diamond rings, and pink Cadillacs to the winners of her annual selling contests.

Interestingly, several of the fortunes made by American women have been in cosmetics—viz., the late Elizabeth Arden, the late Helena Rubinstein, and the very alive Estée Lauder. Encouragingly, other fortunes are now being accumulated by women in all kinds of businesses and industries that have nothing to do with cosmetics and fashion.

You pay a terrible price for ignorance in any area of your life, and it, of course, becomes glaringly and gallingly evident what the price is when you've undersold yourself. A free-lance writer in Boston told me she had done this when she undertook a complex copy assignment for an insurance company. "I had just moved there from Vermont and didn't know anything about the going rates for copy," Winnie said, "so when I showed them samples of my work and quoted them a price like the ones I'd been getting in my hometown— about a sixth the size of Boston—one of the men in the group jumped at it instantly and put me under contract. I found out later that other writers who can't really organize a project like that one and whose writing is really inferior to mine get almost twice as much as I'm charging. Now I'm unable to get the price adjusted. Worse still, the man who hired me keeps escalating the assignment—and the woman who works as his copy chief rips my writing apart as if I'm a cub instead of a seasoned professional. I get the feeling she thinks I couldn't be much good or my work wouldn't be so cheap."

Could be, Winnie. The man who hired you knows a bargain when he sees it and was eager to take advantage of the opportunity to sign you up. His copy chief is afflicted with the suspicion that there must be a hole in this cheap merchandise somewhere and is determined to find it.

Women have often been hired precisely because they were willing to work for less money and, equal opportunity laws notwithstanding, this still goes on. Some of the most profitable work experiences I ever had began because I was willing to "start cheap." There is an inherent trap in this strategy, however, since it is often difficult to negotiate the change in status that can win you a salary increase, as Winnie found out. It is the duty of "good managers" to get as much as they can for the company's money. This includes your salary, and a lot depends on how they handle you—in short, on how well they can get you to perform at a given salary and under a given set of circumstances. It is, in turn, your duty to yourself to get as much of the company's money as you can in return for whatever you are willing to give. This is seldom easy—for the manager or the managee.

A woman in Nashville complained to me last October that she took a job as an administrative assistant because the company (a hardware manufacturer) has an excellent national reputation, is obviously flourishing, and appeared to be a promising place to make rapid progress.

"So far," she said, "it's been promising all right—but the promises haven't materialized. The personnel department assured me I could advance to a manager's job, which would pay more money and provide more perks, but the head of my division keeps putting me off. The manager of the department I'm in left two months ago but I'm doing his work without the title or the salary that goes with it. I asked the division head about it but he said let's wait and see—whatever that means."

What that means is this: the longer she does a manager's job at an administrative assistant's pay, the better the division's record will look. She had applied for the job when the former manager left. What she should do next is talk to the division head again, remind him pleasantly but firmly that she was promised a managerial position when she joined the company, that she has been doing the manager's job since he left, and that she must be told now what the next step is—when she may expect the promotion or whether she should ask Personnel for relocation. If this doesn't get a commitment, she should tell her boss she loves working for him but would like his blessing to request a transfer from Personnel. Needless to say, all this should be done in a nonhostile, friendly manner. Nobody should hate you for doing the best you can for yourself as well as the company. Be friendly about it, but firmly resolved.

In Cleveland, another woman was equally unhappy because she had gone into the administrative area of a food company that had a reputation for "fast executive mobility." Millie had big ambitions and high hopes. "I've worked my tail off," she said, "and I know I've done a really outstanding job because everybody says so. My supervisor never misses an opportunity to compliment me but never takes an opportunity to promote me—and there have been several, one just two weeks ago when a manager left. Also, I never get more than a routine salary increase."

What had she done about it? Millie looked bewildered and a little indignant. "Why, not anything," she said. "They all know what I can do! They all know what a big contribution I'm making! They should give me what I'm entitled to without my having to go in and degrade myself by asking for it!"

I think they should come across, too, Millie. But I do not think there is anything degrading about a frank and open discussion of compensation for one's time, skill, and energy. "But I don't *like* to talk about money!" Millie said. "It's gauche!" Gauche or not, it's what business is about. It is the vaunted Bottom Line that management lives by because it is life or death to the company and up or out to the people who are responsible for it.

Some companies are not operated for immediate profit and these attempt to make up for a weak "cash position" by offering compensation other than money. Ditto for others in situations that breed unpredictable Bottom Lines. If you work for one of these where the money is iffy, be sure you get the optional compensations.

Pat in Miami works for a management consulting firm whose owner is away much of the time conducting seminars and promoting the books he writes. The firm is underdeveloped and probably will continue to be unless the owner is "cloned." Pat says, "I'm not getting rich here but it suits me right down to the ground. I can schedule my own hours and get time off whenever I want it. The boss is very generous about that and about bonuses, too. My salary is nothing to write home about but I get nice surprises—unexpected bonuses. He says it's always feast or famine around here and when it's feast time I get an extra check."

The trouble with that is the difficulty Pat has in budgeting her salary. Since she works for a man who cannot project his company's income, neither can she project hers. She laughs. "I budget as if my salary is all there'll be. I don't count on the bonuses and when they come through, I just look on them as money in the bank. I'm not very good at saving on my own so it works out fine."

Whatever works. The object is to get whatever it is you want or need from a job at the time. If what you want is freedom to come and go on a reasonable schedule of your own, so be it. If it's money, and a lot of it, and if it isn't coming through on the promised or expected timetable, don't hesitate to initiate a friendly discussion—remembering that there's a vast difference between a friendly discussion and a belligerent confrontation.

It is amazing to realize that there are still men around who sincerely subscribe to the same theory about women and money that the early settlers held about Indians and whiskey: "Makes 'em crazy!" I heard this philosophy expounded at length by a key executive in one of the nation's largest retail chains. This is a corporation headquartered in New York but rooted in nineteenth-century attitudes toward women. Until 1976 there had never been a female vice-president on the premises and the one so blessed is a token with title only, inasmuch as her salary and voice are in no way equal to those of the male V.P.s—and are, in many cases, substantially less than those of untitled men. Although it is estimated that over 80 percent of the company's goods are bought by women, management clings to a low opinion of the gender.

"The trouble with giving women salary increases," said the company philosopher, "is they throw their money away. Here in New York a girl who gets a raise blows it on a new apartment or something like that. A man will invest it in a home for his family over in New Jersey or increase his insurance; something sensible like that!"

I quoted him to one of the women on his executive staff, who replied: "He meant every word of it, too— and worse still, that was practically an explanation of company policy. I've been head of a major department here for seven years and my salary is exactly one third that of the man who holds the identical job in another division. When I had exhausted all other avenues of approach toward a reasonable salary adjustment, I finally pointed this out—only to be told that the difference was due to the difference in the volume of our departments. My job is every bit as difficult and demanding as his and I can't help feeling that if my gender were the same as his, our paychecks would be more similar."

Why didn't she quit? This is one of those corporations that uses the carrot technique to best effect in keeping personnel in place—i.e., they have alluring benefit packages that pay off at retirement. "In three more years," she said, "I'll be vested and that will make a big difference in what I take out of the company when I leave. If I go now, I stand to lose too much. Seven years ago when I came here, I was married to a big earner and my own salary wasn't too important. I came in at a low figure because I really wanted the job, which is creative and which I've been able to use to explore my own ideas in spite of the arch conservatism here. Now that I'm divorced, my salary is critical—but salaries here are based on grades and mine started low. Raises are given according to a strict percentage formula on a years-of-service basis only. Performance doesn't count, except consistently bad performance. And there's also something called moral turpitude, which can get you fired and play hell with your benefits."

Would she take a noncreative job at a higher salary if she were starting out now unmarried? "Probably not. I am bored out of my mind by most routine and am not happy doing things the same old way. However, there are other creative jobs in my field that I am equipped to do and should have applied for years ago instead of becoming complacent."

This woman finally did get up the courage to walk away from the carrot and set up shop as a retail consultant. Her income now so far exceeds the salary she was getting that the retirement benefits she would have gained by staying fade into insignificance.

My own attitudes toward money are based on an amusing piece of advice I got from a shoe buyer at one of the stores where I worked early in my career as an advertising manager. The sage shoe man, who had been with the same store all of his working life, whispered to me one day: "When you work for this bunch, you have to ask them for a raise every time you pass by them to keep them from cutting your pay!"

I knew that he was being funny but I also knew that a nucleus of truth was buried in his whispered one-liner. I have not made a practice of asking for a raise every time I passed by them, but I have always let my employers know that money meant as much to me as it did to them. People at the top seldom mind your healthy interest in your own income, knowing that in order to do as well as you can for yourself, you'll do well by them, too! Again, it is the men—and now some women —in middle management to watch out for. They are, as already noted, unprotected and discontented. They are nervous about their own showing as managers, which includes their ability to motivate you. They are tense about making optimum use of their departmental budgets and frightened over the consequences of exceeding them. Above all, they are anxious about that Bottom Line, eager for it to be so big and black that there'll be more money for them. Lacking top management's overview, they may invoke some foolish "economies." When you encounter one of these, it is important to be firm about your own salary goals and to make it clear that you will leave if these are not met. A large word of caution: be *prepared* to leave when you say so and be sure to make an unemotional statement rather than a threat. Either have another job definitely waiting in the wings—or have enough money squirreled away to keep you going while you look around. Overeager "new" bosses can make strange decisions.

Six weeks ago, a woman I know who had just become sales promotion manager for a small manufacturer of radio components in Connecticut told me she was having staff problems.

"Already they're hitting on me for raises," Marie said. "Nobody got one last year when they were supposed to because the man who just left was worried about losing his job and wanted to keep cost of operations down. Well, they were all waiting for me and, one by one, they've demanded more money. I'm not particularly concerned about any of them except the art director, who is exceptional and a real bargain. I think I can keep him at the same salary for at least six months though, and instead of handing out raises, I'm going to use the money to do an extra trade promotion and try to start off with a terrific splash! Maybe get a ten-thousand-buck raise for myself! Neat, huh!?"

As the situation developed, it was not so neat. The next time I saw her, she told me the art director had quit. "He said he 'felt exploited' and wouldn't stay on at any price," she said with a tinge of irony. "Oh, well—art directors are all nuts anyway. The one I hired was godawful, not even worth what I was paying him."

Marie had graded the job down to reduce her salary
budget still more. When the new art director bombed,
"the whole creative group started doing a lousy job"
and Marie's department became thoroughly demoral-
ized. She was fired and is convinced that it was a sexist
matter rather than a result of her own awkward way of
handling the budget.

Marie, of course, erred in trying to save her department's salary budget instead of investing it in the people who could have helped her make that "terrific
splash." Companies are used to investment spending,
having been engaged in it since they started. If the
object of their owners was to save money, they
wouldn't be in business at all. They'd have their capital
socked away in high-interest bonds, gold, real estate, or
whatever appears to offer the biggest yield. Instead,
they have chosen to invest it in themselves, their businesses, and, if you work there, you. If they have given
you a budget, they fully expect it to be spent.

This does not mean that you should act like a sailor
on shore leave or spend it up immediately, to the last
dime. The spending should be thoughtful and respect-
ful because, although it is earmarked as yours, it belongs to somebody else. One man I know habitually
refers to dollars in his budget as chips and it drives me
crazy. I also break out in blisters when money is called
bread. I have never heard anyone who had a significant
amount of it refer to money as anything except exactly
what it is: money.

If you find yourself in a situation comparable to
Marie's, by all means keep the key people (like the
exceptional art director) happy and working. He might
have felt marked down already to be suddenly working

for a woman when he had been hired by a man, and to deny him a long-awaited salary increase could make his position intolerable. Actually, you should try to keep all hands on deck until you've had a chance to evaluate their performance in terms of the situation. There's no point in trying to buy their loyalty with instant raises all around. You'll only look like a patsy and, worse still, scared. Do have a talk with each of them the first day, explain that you're analyzing the department, sizing the whole thing up. Assure them that you will discuss salary with them and talk to them about work details—right away. Be sure that it *is* right away and, if there's one person you especially need, make it tomorrow.

It's important to be "upfront" about it. If there really is no money for raises and you can't get any appropriated at the moment, explain this but say you will do all that you can to change matters the moment the profit picture changes—and mean it. Also, let them know you need their help and are counting on it. There is something wonderful about being needed that most people respond to.

In Memphis a woman who works for a large pharmaceutical house told me about a "speech" delivered to the department by a new female boss—to her extreme detriment and ultimate downfall. "You never heard such popping off in your life," she said. "Ms. Biginsky told us how great she is and what miracles she expected to accomplish. The idea was that if we stuck with her and did exactly as she said, we might be around to kiss her ring at the Christmas party. She also warned us that we should expect no change in salary or status until we proved ourselves to *her*." Needless to say, "Biginsky" doesn't work there anymore. She not only failed to get anybody's cooperation, she was ignominiously sabotaged in a lot of little ways that made her look bad.

I hope she learned from the experience. A Philadelphia woman I met at a seminar certainly did. She had the courage to recount her experience in taking over the operation of her husband's meat-packing business after he had died suddenly of a heart attack. "I was confused, bitter, and terrified," she said. "I knew a little bit about the business from having listened to my husband's plans and problems, but I hadn't worked in it—hadn't worked anywhere for twelve years, although I had been an accountant before I got married.

"Well, the first thing I did was horrendous. I called a meeting of the executive staff—all men—and told them I was having to take over because they had killed my husband by not doing their jobs right and I planned to run things differently. That they could get on the ball or get out of the ball game because I had no intention of letting them kill me. I also announced that I was wiping out the executive incentive plan because my husband had been overgenerous and I had three children to educate." Wow!

"Naturally, they quit," she continued, "and I told myself it was because they couldn't stand the idea of working for a woman. I had hell putting a staff together and finally realized nobody could stand working for *that kind* of woman."

Nothing except her competence is more important to a woman in business, whether as boss or employee, than her credit rating—which is something to guard with your life. Regrettably, a great many people who should know better still regard women as poor credit risks—not necessarily less trustworthy, but less likely to have the money at pay-up time. In the light of past access to money, this is as understandable as it is regrettable.

When I had been operating my own business for two years and set out to lease new office space in midtown Manhattan, I was asked by the building's manager if Mr. D'Agostino, who was my principal client, would "guarantee" my rent payment. I replied, rather testily, that I would guarantee it myself, and the building manager (also a woman, representing a female real estate owner) reluctantly leased the space to me without the requested endorsement. "You know how it is . . ." she said. And I do, indeed, know how the attitude is. The double standard does linger in both sexes, nowhere more clearly than in money matters. Forfeiture of debts by men is never (repeat, never) attributed to gender; in almost any debt defection by women, gender is immediately cited.

It is often inconvenient and sometimes disadvantageous to pay bills the moment they become due. There are companies whose payments lag from three to five months, on account of "the backlog of work" or deliberate policy adopted to permit extended use of capital. Companies whose expenditures run to millions can gain substantial leverage this way—and so can individuals who follow rich, beautiful life-styles. All of us know nauseatingly wealthy people (and people who like to look that way) who make a practice of paying bills quarterly, semiannually, or even annually, and it seems to work well for them. Just don't count on it. A dazzling credit rating is an endearing plus.

As for "white collar crime," reported to be on the
rise among women as their numbers at work increase, it
goes without saying that you stay out of that.

A New York woman who, along with two men, was
indicted early in 1980 on charges of having defrauded
the Small Business Administration and several banks of
$10.5 million clearly has what it takes for legitimate
accomplishment. In the gleeful press reports about the
indictment, her gender has been heavily underscored—
the more so, perhaps, because the stated purpose of her
company was to assist women in obtaining funds from
the SBA to launch small businesses and otherwise guide
them through the start-up.

She bitterly insists that she was victimized by a man
in the D.A.'s office who was burning to make a name
for himself and by other men who are unwilling to
accept the fact that a woman could accomplish what
she did—which included acquisition of impressive properties and the handling of huge sums of money. Regardless of the outcome, the indictment will probably
remain a deterrent to women in business, who, like it or
not, must (to coin a cliché) be like Caesar's wife—i.e.,
"above reproach." The woman's case was not helped by
reports in the press that one of the men indicted along
with her is a disbarred attorney.

If this book seems overly concerned about money, it
is because the subject of it is business—and the object
of business is to make money. Whether money is your
principal motivation for working or not, here are some
considerations:

1. *Don't sell yourself short.* Since our society
does equate value with cost, you may be valued

in direct ratio to what you're being paid. Be sure it's enough.

2. *Before putting a price on your services, find out the industry norm for your locale.* Weigh this against what you have to offer and establish your own asking point accordingly, plus or minus.

3. *Psych yourself up to negotiate.* Smother your mother's attitudes about the unfeminine nature of interest in money and show a healthy interest in earning your share.

4. *Examine your company's benefits package carefully, preferably with a lawyer.* Most of these packages are unbelievably complex, worded in legalese, and almost impossible to fathom if you are not an attorney. Be sure that the package is a really worthwhile aspect of your company before considering it a factor in your length of stay.

5. *Don't expect management to volunteer salary increases and don't feel insulted if they appear minimal.* It is universally regarded as "good management" to get as much as possible for all expenditures, and if the increases do not occur or seem too small, speak up.

6. *When you're in a management role yourself, don't be niggardly with your salary budget and don't be tense about investment spending in any area.* Opportunities missed through overcaution are as damaging to your career as opportunities messed up.

7. *Guard your credit rating with your life and yield not to temptation to pick up a fast, shady buck.* Your gender is always on the line in money matters; fair or not, that's the way it is.

Chapter
8

I
Double-Dare
You!

There is something irresistible about a chip on the shoulder, no matter whose shoulder it's on or how it got there. The temptation to knock it off is overwhelming and most mortals can't resist taking a shot at it. If you take one to the office, be prepared.

Granted, the woods are full of chip material for women. A dog's life is lovely compared to an underdog's, and if you've decided that the underdog lot you inherited along with your gender is not for you in business, congratulations! Just try not to disturb the peace with your intentions.

A chip on your shoulder is not only a threat to other people, it is a threat to the peace. Especially yours. Business rides on confidence and optimism and those who are dearest to management are the ones who project both. A chip on the shoulder means something is

wrong and if you're parading one around, you're parading a problem. The quickest solution may be to get rid of you. (It may not get rid of the problem, but it gets the evidence out of sight.) An aggrieved manner makes management feel guilty and threatened—two emotions that are shattering to those who are supposed to be in control.

The woods are also full of women who are loaded with capability but confined to small status and small salary by their own unwelcome personality traits.

One woman I know has a red-hot temper and is proud of it. "Listen," she says, "I know I've got a short fuse. I come from a long line of fighters and screamers. It's this red hair! When people get on my nerves or do stupid things that cause me trouble, I don't fail to let them know it!" She certainly doesn't. Everybody within a quarter-mile radius can hear what's on her mind when what's there is not very pleasant. And she is glad!

Another woman says, "I'm sorry—but it's just the way I am. When something gets my Irish up, I just have to let it out! Anybody standing around at a time like that is gonna get it. Did you ever know anybody Irish who wasn't like that?"

Answer: yes. Also, I've known many a red-haired woman with an even temperament and pleasant disposition—both of which are decided pluses in most jobs. Maybe a volatile disposition that causes you to erupt like Vesuvius is the way you are—but rewarding or even tolerating erratic (especially belligerent) behavior is not the way business acts. The boss seldom views any belligerence kindly except his own.

I have worked with half a dozen women who had

brilliance, knowledge, talent, skill—and absolutely rotten dispositions. One said she got up mad every morning and got madder as the day went along. Another was a "Doomsday Girl," as full of bad news as a letter from home. Still another was a pouter, usually so morose it made everybody unhappy to look at her. All of them were stuck in meaningless jobs in spite of their extraordinary capabilities—because each was cursed with personality traits that added up to a big, fat chip on the shoulder.

Don't tell me. I know. A lot of men have absolutely rotten dispositions, too. I also know that their chances of getting away with it are so much greater that we can bet without consulting Jimmy the Greek. Don't waste time and emotional energy brooding about it. As a woman who wants to get ahead on male terrain, your own chances are better if you keep your chip to yourself, preferably hidden away in a bottom drawer at home.

The other day I had lunch with a friend who told me about a woman at her company who kept the whole place in an uproar almost all of every afternoon. "The problem with Cindy," she said, "is that she drinks her lunch. She is inclined to be hostile anyway and when she gets a skin full of gin (her favorite tipple), she hyperventilates the hostility. She says she's not getting a fair shake at our place—and probably isn't—but, right or wrong, she drives everybody crazy bitching about it. She goes into the office of first one man and then another and delights in telling them point-blank that she's smarter than any man on the premises and much better at her job. She's got a raucous voice that's even more unpleasant when she's sloshed and you can hear her angry ranting all over the area. Nobody can get much done when Cindy's on the warpath!"

Yesterday, I had lunch with my friend again and she told me that, sure enough, Cindy had been fired.

"Nobody was surprised," she said, "and to tell you the truth, nobody cared. Cindy really is as smart as she thinks she is, and from nine to noon every day when she's sober, she cracked into it and did a super job— which is why she lasted as long as she did. But the hostility was too much for everybody and finally one of the fellows got so annoyed at her for beating up on him when he was racing the clock on an important assignment that he insisted she go with him to the supervisor and make a formal complaint. They went, but Cindy's complaint was hardly formal! She ranted and raved at the top of that grating voice until Mr. Simms (the supervisor) asked her to go home and try to feel better."

Shortly after they left, Mr. Simms sent a messenger to Cindy's apartment with a severance check enclosed in a letter suggesting she would be happier elsewhere. She probably won't be. Someone else who has worked with her says, "Cindy's had a chip on her shoulder so long she'd be lonely without it. I told her that once and I thought she was going to hit me. She glowered at me and finally said 'Goddammit, I've got a right to!' Maybe she has. But what does it get her?"

What it got her in that instance was fired. If Cindy felt discriminated against, she should not have vented her anger and disappointment on her associates. She should have asked Mr. Simms for an appointment and gone to see him alone for a calm, quiet discussion of her credentials. Sans the martini lunch. The details of her job—assignments, work quality, status—should be discussed privately and confidentially. With a "skin full of gin," she hardly had a chance, and with a witness present, Mr. Simms hardly had a choice. Even without the unfortunate confrontation, though, Cindy's future there had to be dim. A large part of her problem was drinking, which she blamed on the fact that she was undervalued as a woman. Whatever the reason, the result was the same. She was disruptive as well as unproductive, on a regular basis, and no company puts up with that indefinitely. A smooth flow of production is essential to profitable operation.

Gigi, who shared an office with a young copywriter I know at a giant ad agency, was a towering talent, seething inside because she was writing soap ads instead of The Great American Novel, that elusive *oeuvre* everybody who writes for a living intends to create "one of these days when I have the time." Gigi did not suffer in silence. She accepted a hefty paycheck for her time and talent, but loudly denounced the agency for "wasting" them. The chip on her shoulder got bigger and bigger, her criticism of the company got louder and louder, until finally the agency creative director (a woman) called her in for a farewell talk.

"You know what the old bitch had the temerity to tell me?" Gigi reported. "That I'm a bad influence. That before I got there she had a happy, productive department. She said I had '*infected*' at least half of them with my cynicism, turning them into 'malcontents' who think their work is 'malicious waste.' Made me feel like Typhoid Mary. Anyway, she was complimentary about

my writing. Said maybe I should be writing other
things since I seem to have a chip on my shoulder
about advertising, and she was giving me the freedom
to 'investigate options' by terminating my job."

Gigi didn't want her job terminated. Neither did she
want to shut herself away from the camaraderie of her
agency friends to invoke the self-discipline of working
alone. Gigi longed to be an author, but was unwilling to
write a book. She didn't want to write "soap copy," but
she did want the money. The frustration of it all gave
her an attitude that translated to the creative director
as a chip on her shoulder. Nobody in management ever
wants the troops to feel that their work is a waste of
time and talent, and the carrier of that little germ is
quickly whisked away by an astute executive.

Women who ascend to positions of authority frequently feel vulnerable. With reason. Since female
authority is still relatively new outside the home and
classroom, a woman executive may find herself tested
so consistently that she starts going into routine business situations with guns blazing. While it's absolutely
necessary to be armed (with information), more armor
than a crisp, firm manner comes off as a chip on the
shoulder—particularly to men.

A woman I know went into a new job last year as
vice-president in charge of purchasing for a furniture
manufacturer. "I can laugh about it now," she says,
"but it was excruciatingly unfunny at first. I had a
strike against me when I went in because I'm a 'dam-
yankee' (the company is in North Carolina), but since
a lot of the people we do business with are in the East,
that wasn't too bad. However, strike two was terrible. I

was a woman in a man's job, in a man's industry, in a part of the country where women's lib was still a dirty joke.

"I'm sorry to tell you I overreacted. I was tested all day, every day, by every man I talked to. My authority was questioned. My decisions were questioned. My facts and figures were questioned. Until finally I got sick of it and started mowing down every man who walked into my office before he said a word."

It worked. They not only stopped questioning her authority, decisions, and information, they stopped talking to her altogether. They refused to go in to see her or telephone her, on the grounds that she had a chip on her shoulder. She couldn't function, so she resigned. But she learned from the experience. The head of the furniture company where she had worked was a wise and wealthy man who could afford to be understanding and sympathetic. He helped her relocate and gave her some sage advice about crossing the gender barrier. "Relax a little," he said. "Keep cool. Be pleasant. Be patient. Answer the questions and as soon as they find out you know what you're talking about and mean what you say, the questioning will stop." That's the way it's worked out.

Last year I had occasion to meet with a group of young women who have been employed as salespeople in the aluminum industry. Selling aluminum products —coils, panels, and all that—was an activity open only to men until the midseventies. The purpose of the meeting I attended was to explore ways for these women to move up into management. This was a bright, energetic group, very ambitious and determined.

One of them, about thirty, said, "Our company policy concerning women is okay at the top, but some of the middle men in management—the ones whose attitudes have direct effect on us—don't exactly follow the stated policy. To lay it out for you, my boss is the sales manager for the division I'm in and I know for a fact he doesn't like the idea of having women on the sales staff because he's said so. I've got a good record—better than three of the four men—but he pretty much ignores me. How do I get around that?"

"It's a big company," I said. "Ask for a transfer."

"I've done that," she replied. "And they said there are no openings. I know that there are so I have to assume that they just don't want to move me. Maybe they hope I'll quit."

"Maybe you're right," I said. "In that case take your experience to another company. People who can really sell are very valuable and much in demand."

She bristled. Up went the chip!

"Why the hell should I have to move because of some stupid, bigoted male chauvinist pig?"

The answer to that is: of course, she shouldn't have to move. But since she can't change his attitude or change her location to another department, the realistic option is to change companies. She's young enough. Smart enough. And her track record is certainly good enough. The only thing she lacks is a handle on reality.

Few collisions with reality have been more devastating to the women involved in them than the clashes brought about by class-action lawsuits. The brave souls who had stood up and fought these legal battles deserve all the applause, all the honor and glory they are getting, for God knows they have got little else. A few months ago I had a conversation with a woman who had won a sex discrimination case in court eight years before but, to date, had "not collected a dime."

"It's cost me a fortune," she said. "In lawyers' fees and in all the time spent haggling in court or preparing to haggle in court. But I'm glad I did it and I'm going to keep on." She's hanging in there—but hanging by the thumbs, making a living outside the corporate structure, writing books and making vituperative lectures.

The company she sued is one of the largest in her industry. She must know that this firm will keep her case in the courts forever and for six months thereafter with appeal after appeal. "They have to win in the long run," I told her. "Fighting a corporation that vast in a case with so many far-flung ramifications is like fighting the telephone company. They'll keep pouring money into the case and sending in fresh platoons of legal eagles from that floor full of lawyers they employ until you, your funds, and your attorney are totally exhausted."

She shrugged. "I don't give a damn," she said. "This whole business of putting women down has got to be changed. I don't have time to wait for the change."

I earnestly hope that makes sense to her, although it makes none at all to me. A huge chunk of her life has already been squandered fighting this windmill, and if her lawsuit has changed anything, the change is negligible. Women who have filed class-action suits have made themselves virtually unemployable and are dismissed from any consideration by the male business establishment as "the suers" (read, sewers). The changes they have sued for cannot possibly benefit them personally and it is doubtful that the female sex in total has benefited, as has been loftily contended. Women progress in business for exactly the same reason men do. They make themselves valuable to a company or to an individual who matters. When a significant number of women have done that, the whole sex will profit as a result. It's more difficult than it ought to be, sure. Men do get the breaks, sure. Unfair? Why debate it? Whoever said life was fair anyway?

I have watched some of the more obstreperous self-appointed leaders of the Women's Revolution in action, and I have watched other people watch them on television. I have seen viewers of both sexes turn away saying, "Whatever *they're* for, I'm *against!*" This emphatically does not apply to the sane, even-handed women who press the cause of gender equity, who push for the passage of E.R.A. in an intelligent, understandable manner. It is the Loud Uglies who have set women in business back and made the quest for gender equality appear ridiculous.

Dismaying and disruptive as a bellicose attitude is, pouting can be as bad, or worse. Pouting is passive aggression, extremely difficilt to deal with—which is one reason why it is used so often and why management hates it beyond almost any other form of resistance. It is the classic ploy of people who feel that they are in exploitable or otherwise disadvantageous situations. Situations which they also feel powerless to change. This describes the historic plight of women and children, who are grouped together by our culture. ("Women and children first!") Therefore, when a woman pouts, it's childish.

Men frequently retreat into frozen silences to indicate disapproval of something that is going on or not going on at work, and the silences are accepted as such. Women who behave the same way are said to be pouting. They're "being childish." They've "got a chip on the shoulder."

In Dallas a man who heads a conglomerate told me that a female executive in one of his companies has "just one terrible trait" that he can't cope with. "I don't understand it," he said. "She pouts. When something displeases her, she clouds up and clams up. Won't say anything to anybody and God alone knows what's wrong. It makes people uncomfortable and nervous— and it's tough on everybody around her. She's one of our most capable executives and except for that I'd say she's superb. I wanted to make her head of a division last year but that stopped me. You just can't have that kind of behavior at that level."

In Cleveland Jean missed a promotion she expected last summer and didn't understand why, but her associates do. One of them told me, "Jean is a pouter. She does a wonderful job, but when something or somebody makes her unhappy, she goes into this big silent spell. All you can get out of her in the way of conversation is a curt 'good morning' and 'good night' and the bare minimum necessary to the day's work—all very short and snappy. Nobody knows what she's peeved about, so everybody feels guilty until she finally breaks down and announces who did what. It's too bad, because she's

very good at her job, works hard, and deserves a promotion."

"Why don't you tell her?" I asked.

"Tell her! Are you kidding? She'd pout with me from
now on!"

Unhappily, some people who have had to fight hard
for top management positions adopt fighting as a way
of life and aggressive behavior as a symbol of office.
Trudy did this after winning a power struggle with a
man at the travel agency where they both worked. The
national company that owned the agency had made
them co-directors when each applied for the job after it
opened up unexpectedly. This is a piece of corporate
stupidity that sometimes happens when two people are
felt to be "equally qualified" and those who are responsible for making a decision aren't able to reach a meeting of minds.

When the man wearied of the struggle and left to
open his own agency, Trudy triumphantly called a
meeting and blasted the whole staff, telling them in
Marine-sergeant language that she had broken an intimate part of her anatomy to occupy that position in
solitary splendor and from now on things were going to
be done her way—or else! She was promptly "or elsed."
One by one they quit, leaving Trudy in a bind for experienced help, and to her chagrin, three of them went
to work for her old adversary in his new enterprise.
"The crazy dame has a chip on her shoulder!" one of
them complained. "She let us know she intended to
push us around—and who needs it!"

Since the need was on Trudy's side, she should have
called the meeting but let it be known that the only real

change would be a move into peace and harmony. She had won the power struggle and it would have been much more statesmanlike to show benevolence toward her departing competitor, to wish him well and express confidence in the staff's capability and loyalty.

The ability to "get along with people" is highly rated by corporations and is one of the first traits cited as a mark of leadership. A chip on your shoulder can remove you immediately from the promotion list, and if you want to be seriously considered for an executive spot, here are some tips about the chips:

1. *Smile.* Unless something devastating has happened that would make anything except a serious countenance totally jarring, give yourself a public beauty treatment: smile. It's relaxing for you and everyone who's looking. An instant face-lift!

2. *Don't take any action in anger, and try not to say a word until you cool off.* A rare explosion can be dramatically effective, but as a rule you get more attention with an unemotional approach.

3. *State your objections and disagreements calmly and courteously,* backed by all the logic and facts you can muster. Emotional outbursts will be ignored as what they are: emotional outbursts.

4. *Never make an issue of small things.* Go along with picayune points when you can do it without damaging a project or your own position; then when you do make an issue of something, it stands out.

5. *Don't pout.* If you don't like something, say so, clearly and firmly, to someone who can change

it. Pouting might have worked for you at home and
may still work there, but at the office it's unpro-
fessional. And childish. Management may do something to appease you provided your work is good,
but your pouting will give them reason not to move
you up.

6. *If you feel hostile, hide it; if gin brings out
your hostility, don't drink it; if you feel superior to
men (or women) around you, don't say so.* You're
not working to win a popularity contest and you're
not out to inherit the ax of Carry Nation, but
neither are you there to win the Bitch of the Year
Award. It's nice to be nice.

7. *Radiate confidence and optimism.* The people
who are investing their money and/or time, talent,
and energy in a project like to feel that it's going
to work. If you think it won't, say so and say why
—but having said it, do all that you can to make it
work anyway!

Chapter
9

Mayday, SOS, and Plain Help!

Are women natural enemies of each other, like the cobra and the mongoose? Or is the historic rivalry between them only cultural—not inherent in the genes but embedded in the mores of society? True, from the cradle to the grave, women do compete with each other for male affection, favor, attention, approval, and sponsorship, sensing that in a man's world a woman gets what the men in her orbit want her to have. "The idea," says an executive woman in Chicago, "is to make them want you to have it!"

I do not know about the validity of her philosophy, but I do know that, in business, the quickest way "to make them want you to have it" is to make it profitable for them. I have observed, too, that women, acting out of the insecurity of Second Sexism, have lacked confidence in their ability to do this—despite dramatic evi-

dence to the contrary! Women do not trust themselves and therefore do not trust each other. Here and there the walls of doubt *are* tumbling down, but the distrust lingers.

From sea to shining sea, I have asked female executives (present and future) to tell me what, in their opinion, is the biggest mistake women in business make. High on every list, and at the very top of many, is: they don't help each other. Some put it a great deal more strongly. In Seattle one said: "They stab you in the back!" In Dallas: "They want to be the only woman around who has any authority." In Memphis: "They find out all they can from you and then use it against you to get ahead." In Baltimore: "Once they get a little status of their own, they do all they can to hold other women back." In Washington: "They play up to the men and help them along every chance they get—but never do a thing for women."

A male executive in Atlanta laughed when I quoted these complaints to him and said, "That's the sort of thing that goes on all day every day among men and nobody's surprised. Just change the sex in those gripes and you've got it! Except it's at least ten times bloodier! Why should women feel that competition at the office is some kind of tea party? That's Down-the-Rabbit-Hole thinking—Alice in Wonderland stuff!"

Women are, indeed, surprised when the competition turns rough and are particularly disappointed when they do not get preferential or at least equal treatment from female associates. Last November a woman at a Cleveland club meeting expressed her dismay like this: "My boss is a woman. She is very smart and everybody knows it, but I think she's a lousy boss because she shows partiality. She likes men and I don't blame her. So do I! But I don't think that's any excuse for giving them every break. They get all the plums in our department. The best assignments. First choice in vacation time and days off. First crack at the promotions and raises. If there's an executive opening anywhere in the company and she's asked for candidates from her group, they're always 'her boys.' I don't think she's ever recommended a woman. One of the girls who got disgusted and quit told her so right to her face and she just said, 'I'm sorry you feel that way. I don't think you understand what kind of spot I'm on.'"

Women who ascend to executive positions do feel that they are "on the spot." Rightly so, because all executives *are* on the spot and women are probably more so. In the matter of promotions and raises they are heavily inclined to "play it safe," giving preference to the people who they believe will remain with the company and prove that their own executive judgment is sound. It is not a bit unusual for an executive to be called upon to justify his or her decisions, and since it is still easier to justify promotions and salary increases for men than for women, it is not a bit unusual for the voice of authority, male or female, to speak up for men. Add to that the fact that the men are usually quicker to speak up for themselves and the stage is set for charges of favoritism.

The other side of the coin was flipped at me in Miami, where a young man complained that his female boss "won't give a man the time of day." He said he was a victim of reverse discrimination. "Talk about chauvinist pigs," he snorted. "She certainly is a female chauvinist pig! I wouldn't be here if I hadn't already been in the department when she came to the company. She won't hire anybody but girls and admits it. Says she's been discriminated against by men and now that she's got a chance to get even, she intends to!"

Although wanting to "get even" is entirely human, it isn't very smart. Executives are prized for their ability to make cool, impersonal decisions, and the fact that most decisions are neither does not alter the fantasy. It is important to *look* cool and impersonal, and the woman who permits herself to become a target for charges of gender discrimination—either way—is in trouble.

The rim of that same coin showed up in Houston, where a former woman executive told me that the adjective "former" was a result of her having tried too hard to show impartiality. "I was determined that nobody would ever accuse me of being unfair to men or women either and I guess you could say I leaned over backward—too far. There were six people in my group and I decided that there would always be an equal division between the sexes. Always three men and three women. Well, the best woman in the group left. We tried to keep her but another company offered her more money than we could match, and a vice-presidency. A man with excellent credentials applied for the vacancy and everything inside me told me he would be perfect. But that would have upset the gender balance so I hired a woman whose qualifications were 'iffy.' I was sorry almost immediately because the next week one of the men in my group decided to move to San Francisco. By then the young fellow I had wanted to hire when I took on the 'iffy' girl had taken another job. Then I guess I panicked. To fill the new male vacancy, I took on the first likely man who applied. Too quickly, because I was disturbed by the two big unexpected changes and wanted to get things settled down. As it developed, things were anything but settled down. Both of the new people bombed totally and, as a result of that, so did the project we were working on. A very important one! My vice-president called me in and said they valued me highly as a worker but felt that I was in over my head as a manager.

"I explained about the two people who screwed up the detail but he pointed out that being able to assemble a good staff is an important part of being an effective executive. When I told him about the gender balance, he said that was admirable but that 'you might as well fall flat on your face as lean too far over backward.' I wasn't fired but I was eased into another nonexecutive spot. I didn't get a salary cut either, but I doubt that I'll ever make much more here."

Having been in the business world for over thirty years, I have worked with (and for) more stepmothers than godmothers but I am pleased to see a turnabout taking place. As more and more women enter the work force and both sexes grow accustomed to the idea of executive women, we can look for happier give and take within the female ranks as well as between the genders.

In New Orleans at a 1979 luncheon of the American Women in Radio and Television, I was impressed by the immediate responsiveness of the membership to an announcement that one of the luncheon guests was "new in town and looking for a job." One member volunteered on-the-spot information about job openings in a new company just starting up, and several others asked her either to see them after the meeting or to phone them at the office.

Aggie Isacks, who was program chairman of the chapter at the time, said, "That's one of the good things we do. We keep our membership filled in on job openings and also on people who are new in the job market or want to make a change. It's a big help all around—to companies on the lookout for personnel, too."

The New Orleans AWRTs were practicing a form of networking that I experienced first as a member and subsequently as president of the Advertising Women of New York. I have also seen it in operation by and for the Women in Communications, Inc., the New York Women's Forum, the Home Economists in Business, the Business and Professional Women's Club, The Fashion Group, the National Home Fashions League, and the YWCA. All of them maintain either formal or informal career counseling programs, and most of their members have been generous in sharing information and skills. Because I have been the beneficiary of their assistance on numberless occasions, I have enormous regard for these organizations and the women who are willing to devote time and energy to the activities they sponsor for the professional advancement of both sexes. They can—and will—get you the answer to almost any business question immediately. If it's not at their fingertips, they will put you in touch with the fingertips where it is.

"Networking" has become one of the current buzz

words and is a hot topic for seminars, magazine articles, and books meant to plug women into a system similar to the much-discussed "old boys' network." In her excellent book called *Networking*, Mary Scott Welch defines it as "the process of developing and using your contacts for information, advice and moral support as you pursue your career." Welch goes on to say, "It's linking the women you know to the women they know in an ever-expanding communications network. It's building a community of working women, across professional and occupational lines outside the old boys' network."

This, as Welch acknowledges, is the major problem with women's networks: they are outside the old boys' network, the hallowed hookup that runs, in one way and another, everything. Early in her book she points out that "a good networker uses every resource available to her, *and that includes men*." The italics are mine because the importance of men to your career cannot be overstated. They still have at least 95 percent of the power—remember? Less than 5 percent of managers earning over $25,000 are women.

So what can other women in business do for you? Plenty. For starters, they can exchange ideas with you on coping with the unique problems of an executive woman—those seemingly small, yet critical, little things that crop up all day to make life difficult and tiresome in matters that are merely routine for an executive man. Things as apparently picayune as what to wear. (This is a subject so nettlesome that whole books are written about it and one, "based on research," has become a best-seller—in spite of the fact that it contains such absurdities as a recommendation that the female executive wear a maroon fedora with a little feather, the kind of hat that looks best on a musical comedy horse.) Things like traveling with male associates, drinking with them, lunching or dining with them, and catching the check when it's high time you did.

These are niggling, personal details but women can also help you shine on the professional front. Their organizations can provide you opportunities to exercise gifts you never get to use on your job, discover talents you didn't suspect you had, grow in new directions, embark on a new career, or gain stature in the career you have. *And* they can also introduce you to the right men. That remains essential. Men *are still the big shot-callers.*

One reason why men continue to call an overwhelming majority of the shots is that women ask them to. Women turn to men for decisions they ought to be making themselves. This includes career decisions and accounts for a lot of the discontent in the female work force. Brothers, fathers, husbands, lovers, male friends, and assorted other sages almost invariably advise women who consult them about job problems to take a course of action that agrees with their own particular ideas of femininity.

Women ask men what kind of cars to buy, what insurance, what stocks and bonds, what stereos, radios, and television sets. This, in spite of the fact that mountains of consumer information are available to guide women in making their own choices on the basis of facts alone. While there are undoubtedly men in your life who base their recommendations to you on facts,

there are just as undoubtedly others who don't know
any more about the subject at hand than you do but
feel constrained to measure up to your expectations by
making something up.

It is always flattering to be asked for advice, and
most people, male or female, cannot resist the temptation to feign expertise. Evidently one of the toughest
utterances in the English language is "I don't know!"
and it gets tougher when a man faces the possibility of
having to say it to a woman.

The problem is compounded in business, where men
are expected to know the answer to everything more
taxing than "Where are the paper clips?" and where
nobody expects a woman to know much else. Consequently a lot of women mark themselves and each other
down by turning to men for decisions, ideas, opinions,
and answers that they—or another woman who is responsible for the area involved—could quickly provide.

Veronica, who works for a large bookstore in New
York, was made supervisor of the nonfiction division
when the man who had been in charge there was
moved up to a bigger job. The people who worked in
nonfiction (mostly women) continued to track down
Veronica's predecessor with questions that only she had
the answers to now. He gamely "guessed"—often
wrong—until Veronica invited him to have coffee with
her and laid out the problem for him in an altogether
friendly manner. "I'll appreciate it, Shep," she told him,
"if you'll refer them back to me. You did a wonderful
job and they're used to relying on you for all the answers to everything. Now that you have such an important position, it's not fair for you to be imposed on or

for people to expect you to keep up with all those piddling details you shouldn't be bothered with. Preserve
your infallibility! Send the tormentors back to me. I'm
being paid to deal with them."

Shep was off the hook! He no longer felt obliged to
guess and could refer the questions to Veronica with a
light heart. If Veronica had made a scene about it with
her employees, they would have told each other she
was jealous of her authority and being bitchy.

What if Shep had been obstreperous and uncooperative? That happened to Wilma in Columbus, Ohio,
when her predecessor didn't want to let go of the department she had been hired to supervise, even though
he had been promoted to a job with overall responsibility. He encouraged the people in her department to
bring all their problems to him even though they were
supposed to report to Wilma.

She had the friendly little chat with him—to no
avail. "He stonewalled me!" Wilma said. "Told me he
couldn't help it if people had confidence only in him
and that he certainly wouldn't turn them away when
they felt he was their only reliable source of help!"

Wilma immediately went to see the vice-president in
charge of the whole section. She stated the matter
calmly and quietly—choosing her language carefully
and scrupulously avoiding any phraseology that could
be construed as emotional. "I didn't dare say George
was undermining my authority," she said. "In fact, I
didn't mention authority at all but said I needed
George's support to carry out my responsibility. The
V.P. immediately saw that it was a real problem and
that I wasn't just bitching. He sent a memo to all em-

ployees in the department saying all matters concerning work there were to be taken up with me only, since
Mr. Callahan's new duties did not permit him to devote
time to former duties. A copy of it went to George—
along with a covering memo from the veep saying he
felt strict observance would be helpful to the smooth
operation of both departments and he knew he could
count on George to refer matters concerning mine back
to me." This was an instance in which a woman's request for male assistance was altogether fitting and
proper because the assistance was solicited from the
one person at the company who could make a constructive difference.

The help of men is, undeniably, valuable to women
in business, but it is seldom easy to enlist. This makes it
all the more important for women to give what aid they
can to each other in business. Toward the end of the
seventies, women's business seminars focused on the
need for an ambitious woman to find a male mentor, an
important executive willing to provide guidance, en-
couragement, and assistance in reaching her goals.

Writing in the premier issue of *Savvy*, the first new
women's magazine to hit the newsstands in the eighties,
Kathleen Fury called it Mentor Mania and, in an article
titled "The Search for Mr. Right Goes to the Office,"
discussed the concept without putting her head on the
line to offer any conclusions. Fury wrote that the ori-
gins of Mentor Mania can be traced to a "concern with
women's careers rather than men's," citing a 1976 *New
Yorker* article by Gail Sheehy called "The Mentor Con-
nection: the Secret Link in the Successful Woman's
Life" and the 1977 book, *The Managerial Woman*, in
which co-authors Margaret Hennig and Anne Jardim

advised ambitious women to "look for a coach, a god-father or godmother, a mentor, an advocate."

As Hennig and Jardim suggest, do look. But do not expect to find. Some women are enormously lucky in this respect and I am one of them, having enjoyed for many years the profound guidance and bolstering of a C.E.O. who is blessed with the prerogatives of owner-ship. Most men who are in a position to be effective mentors do not own the company and must concentrate on moving up the corporate ladder themselves. Any protégés they pick are apt to be young comers who can, in turn, be helpful in their own rigorous climb—who can execute pieces of business that are essential to their progress but beneath their status, who can be groomed to take over strategic spots in middle management that could be worrisome, if not detrimental, to the mentor if the job fell into unfriendly hands. Such protégés are almost never female. Generally speaking, women, as the latecomers to business, do not yet have ready access to the contacts and facilities needed to do a major executive's "sensitive work." Consequently, the women whom executive men rely on are almost always their secretaries—period. Their protégés are men who can be helpful to them in ways that their secretaries and young female executives cannot.

Too, there is the low-flying suspicion that swoops down on male-female relationships, regardless of purity and propriety. In the existing corporate structures male protégés are instantly accepted by other executives as so-and-so's Young Turk and respected as such. Young female protégées cause eyebrows to shoot up—in envy or what-the-hell-does-he-see-in-her wonderment.

There are notable exceptions, and one of the most

outstanding is cited by Kathleen Fury in her *Savvy* article. Fury says, "Margaret Mead's relationship with anthropologist Franz Boas, who persuaded her to change her field of study from psychology to anthropology and encouraged her unique perspective, was obviously rewarding. But for every person lucky enough to have a true mentor, there must be hundreds who have gotten their mentoring in fragments from several or many people."

The fact that women usually are required to get their mentoring in this fragmented fashion is probably all to the good, since relying on one man for assistance can be chancy. If the mentor's fortunes decline, he is not in a position to advance the fortunes of anyone else and may himself be casting about for a sponsor to give him a leg up. Dr. Dorothy Gregg, quoted elsewhere in these pages, is also quoted by Fury. She describes her godmother-protégée relationship with Jean Wade Rindlaud, the first woman vice-president of BBDO and a member of that advertising agency's board of directors, adding this, "She gave me a piece of advice I have always followed: Don't have just one but two or three mentors. If one of them loses power, you should be able to move on with another."

Jean Rindlaud, now retired, was a wise and generous ally for a whole generation of career women, at a time when the business climate for them was cool to freezing. Now that it is warming up, even heating up in some quarters, the opportunities to be or to get a fairy godmother are somewhat thicker—but still thin.

Patty O'Toole, author of numerous "think pieces" in the area of business and finance, said this in the October, 1979, issue of *Self*: "I hate the mentor fad because so few people are in a position to go out and get a mentor. Furthermore, thousands of people have succeeded without them; thousands more have gotten ahead by thinking of all competent supervisors as mentors, by learning everything they could from each. Finally, emphasizing the need for mentors gives women one more excuse for not succeeding, one more way to sit on their hands and wait for some corporate Prince Charming to guide and take care of them."

As previously stated, look for but do not expect to find the mentor who can light your path. While you're looking, try these:

1. *Don't try to be one of the boys.* Business doesn't need any more "boys." It needs able, open-minded women who have pride in what they are and what they can do.

2. *Trust yourself.* Your gender has not jellied your brain or otherwise undermined your capability as an achiever outside the so-called comfort and security of home base. Having faith in yourself makes it possible for you to have faith in your gender—to realize that you don't have to be male to succeed in business and neither does anyone else.

3. *Join the club.* Don't hesitate to get together with women who have the same job interests and problems you do. Even though you're "not a joiner," even though you "can't stand women's groups," even though you've been disappointed in an organization before, go ahead and give it a

chance. Just one good idea, one good contact is worth a lot of meeting hours—some of which will be boring, a few extraneous, and most, fattening. (Cheap meals are usually high calorie; club meals usually have to be cheap. Go, but don't eat!)

4. *Having joined, join in.* Recently a woman with a chip on her shoulder larger than she is excoriated me about the Advertising Women of New York. It developed she only went to "a couple of dull meetings" and didn't go back because "they were an unfriendly bunch." Actually, the complainer may be the most hostile human being I've ever met and the Ad Women of New York are among the friendliest. Whatever the prevailing attitude, go in smiling, handshaking, and volunteering. If you don't like the way things are going, work to change them; if you do, work to make them better. In any event, get involved—and work. The ancient saw is still around because it's so: you get out what you put in.

5. *Base your personnel decisions on ability rather than sex.* Gender is an accident, not a credential or a disqualification.

6. *Don't be discouraged if you don't have a mentor—if no top-seeded man springs out to take you by the hand to become your shepherd.* In today's gyrating corporate structures, it can no longer be assumed that a man will move up in a direct line to power and glory—and should a strong man choose you rather than a young male protégé, you could both wind up wound down. In the event that you do find a mentor, don't allow yourself to be-

come a "dependent"—emotionally or otherwise. Watch successful people of both sexes—especially the women—and take your cues from them.

7. *Once you get going up the ladder, don't forget what the lower rungs were like.* A recent Broadway show got a laugh with a line that went something like this: "You don't have to be nice to people on the way up unless you intend to go back down!" Funny? The audience howled—probably out of mass hysteria. Nobody ever intends to go back down. But it happens. . . .

Chapter 10

"Deliver Me from the Politics"

Politics alone can't get you to the top in business, but one thing is certain: you'll never get there without it. Neither will you get any other place you have in mind unless your mind-set finds contentment in minimums. Call it diplomacy, call it compromise, call it whatever goes down easiest, but political savvy by any name is an absolute essential to success. Without it—and the reasonably smooth practice of its basics—you might as well go home and stay there.

Yet over and over and over, like the much-sung broken record, I hear women express distaste for politics, ranging all the way from mild disapprobation to a kill-kill-kill kind of hatred.

In Philadelphia: "I enjoy my job, except for all the political maneuvering and infighting. It's hard to know what's going on from one day to the next because of the

office politics." In Portland: "What I really can't abide
at the place where I work is the politics. Everything
could be so pleasant if it weren't for all the scheming
and manipulation." In St. Louis: "Can you believe it?
Office politics has become so commonplace that a job
applicant asked one of the secretaries at our firm to fill
her in on the political situation. As if that particular
secretary wouldn't be the last to know! Now there's
another one here who'd be the *first* to know because she
learned her way around the jungle from our company
political expert, the V.P. she's always worked for. What
a pair!" In Birmingham: "The outfit I work for is super
in a lot of ways but I'm quitting. It's the crazy, degrading, stupid, time-wasting politics!"

Politics can be all that: crazy, degrading, stupid,
time-wasting, and a lot more that is disconcerting and
reprehensible, but, like death and taxes, it is always
with us. It is even in places where taxes aren't—like
church.

No two ways about it, "politics" has become a dirty
word. The Second International Edition of Webster's
Unabridged Dictionary gives "politics" a twenty-line
definition, concentrating on government and leaning
hard on organization, regulation, and administration.
Business boils it down simply to getting along with
people—and getting things done.

The very first person you've got to get along with is
your boss. No one is more important to your career
than the man or woman who can get you promoted or
get your pay raised. Get along with him or her by all
means—and if you have any contact at all with the
C.E.O. or the person who owns the place, do some
plain and fancy getting along there.

In *How to Succeed in Business Without Really Try-ing*, the deliciously comic satire discussed in Chapter 6, office politics is raised to its ridiculous zenith by the book's protagonist, an ultra-devious young man who is determined to go all the way without working. The theory that this could happen tickled the avarice of a whole generation and its tug at the imagination re-mains with us, because the idea of effortless achieve-ment has universal and deathless appeal. This is prob-ably why so many men profess a preference for luck to any other attribute. "I'd rather be lucky than smart," says one brilliant man of my acquaintance, "because if you're not lucky, it doesn't help to be smart. Or any-thing else!"

Making accomplishment look easy is such an ac-cepted mark of professionalism that most of us enjoy striking wonder into the breasts of onlookers with our facility at whatever we do. "Trying too hard" is roundly damned as the practice of neophytes and fools.

This throws a lot of people off, because nothing (*re-peat, nothing*) is dearer to the heart of a boss than the sight of a worker toiling away at the job. Whatever the circumstances, your boss probably thinks he or she didn't have it too easy and doesn't expect you to have it that way either. Therefore, nothing (*repeat, nothing*) is more politic than looking busy and sounding busy even if what you're up to has no more to do with com-pany business than picking a horse in the fifth race at Belmont. Better, of course, that you should be im-mersed in company matters, but idleness while the meter is running is unforgivable.

In the *How to Succeed* book, Finch (that ultra-devious young man) rushed to the office on Saturday morning before the boss got there, scattered papers all over his own desk, and littered the ashtrays with mounds of cigarette butts. When the boss stuck his head in the door and said, "Good morning," Finch replied, "Oh, is it morning already, sir?"—with predictable results! The boss beamed. The boss got his name. The boss marked him for bigger things!

There are management people around who think you are poorly organized if you have to work overtime. And if yours is one of these, you should be aware of it and act accordingly. Also, there is a recent trend toward deriding "workaholics," but it should be emphasized that the trend is mainly in the media and the seminars —not management. No matter what the magazines and seminar speakers tell you, managements *adore* workaholics and bosses look for employees who are as neurotic and compulsive about work as they are!

You will seldom, if ever, be expected to work all night, but the fact that you would be willing to is indescribably endearing to most managements. Overblown though Finch's performance was, signs of dedication and devotion do earn Brownie points at the office. They're "good politics."

The busy-busy-busy technique was used with remarkable effect by the empire builder I worked for at a large New York advertising agency. (In an earlier chapter I called her Jennifer.) A woman at her level (call *her* Jan) was competing with her for a vice-presidency, and although Jan was a sharper advertising person, she was an inferior politician. Jan had a habit of visiting other offices to describe her problems and the solutions she had found for them. Not Jennifer! Jennifer

never visited another office for any reason unless she
was specificially requested to do so by someone who out-
ranked her. She kept up a steady drumbeat of activity
in her own office and when she wanted to see other
people, depending on their rank, either summoned or
invited them there. With all the meetings and conferences going on in her office, it was the busiest place on
the floor and she dramatized the activity by referring to
it as "the Grand Central Station of the agency." Her
rival rose above it, roaming the corridors looking idle
(although she usually was thinking through a major
concept) while Jennifer looked and sounded like the
Supreme Commander of the Allied Invasion Forces.
Guess which one of them got the vice-presidency?

Not only is "politics" a dirty word, so is a lot of the
language that has grown up around it. The corporate
epithet that always brings out the boxing gloves is
manipulation. In November, 1979, I was on a YWCA
career panel with Barbara Smith, the vice-president
and management supervisor of Ogilvy & Mather, Inc.,
whom I've already quoted in these pages. Our subject
was Positive Manipulation, and Barbara said this:

" 'Manipulation' is an ugly word. Even coupled with
the word 'positive' it has a negative ring. It suggests a
puppet and a puppeteer. One person pulling the
strings, and the other being pulled. I suppose all of us
feel we've been manipulated at some point or another
and when we have, it has not been a pleasant experience. No one wants to be yanked around on the strings
of another."

Barbara went on to discuss manipulating things
rather than people, "maneuvering our careers to iden-

tify opportunity, to seize it, to take charge and to grow
by the experience it provides." Excellent management
strategy!

Additionally, management often requires action directly involving people as well as things. The respectable term for this is Management by Motivation, and
whether you're being manipulated or motivated may
depend on your own point of view or even how you feel
that day. If you are the one doing the manipulating or
motivating, which it is probably depends on your intentions.

Marcia is very upset because she was invited to
lunch several times by a senior vice-president of her
company who encouraged her to talk about the work in
her department, telling her she has a fascinating mind
and that he enjoys hearing her slant on company affairs.
She was flattered and gave him a great deal of information about her boss and the way he operated. Now her
boss has been fired and the department has been placed
under the supervision of the vice-president who was
her confidant. If he still thinks she has a fascinating
mind, he isn't inviting her to lunch to hear her slant on
the new setup.

Marcia feels manipulated—and rightly so. She really
liked her boss and believes he was doing a fine job, but
understands how some of the things she said about the
department might have been used against him.

On the other hand, Helen complained that she felt
manipulated when one of her peers cultivated her
friendship while the friend was working toward a promotion—which she got. "Now she won't have anything
to do with me," Helen complained, "in spite of the fact

that I sang her praises all over the place and really raved about her to the efficiency experts who were in here doing a survey and making recommendations." Actually, her friend was too busy with her new assignment to go shopping with her at lunch or leave at five thirty with her for cocktails as they had done in the past—as Helen eventually realized.

One of the most interesting cases of manipulation I've heard about surfaced last week when a friend—a woman—who is a key executive in a huge conglomerate told me about a visit she had from a black leader, warning her that her company was readying a "new policy about minorities." She said, "He told me they are going to start easing women and blacks out of important jobs and we should cooperate very closely to prevent this. I happen to know that this man leads a group engaged now in trying to protect a black executive here who has taken cynical advantage of his minority status. He makes no effort to assume responsibility and doesn't bother to show up half the time. We've had the same situation here with other minorities—including women—and I believe we help each other more by observing high performance standards and expecting them of each other than by banding together for so-called mutual protection."

Manipulation and Motivation are first cousins at least —if not twins—since they are often indistinguishable, one from the other. They have the same object: to accomplish, prevent, establish, or wipe out something. The difference, as I understand it, is that the wrong kind of manipulation is undertaken for the advantage of the manipulator only—and the hell with the ma-

nipulee!—while in the right kind of motivation, both
parties (or all parties) stand to gain. One of the questions I hear most often everywhere is: "How can people
be motivated?" And the only answer I know to that
one is: "Depends on the people! Find out what they
want and offer it to them in exchange for what they've
got. And be very sure they get it!"

Creating "the right impression" is the part of office
politics that critics of business get violent about, but
since the business critics have no control over what you
want anyway, pay no attention. Your raunchy friends
may urge you to smack your boss in the kisser with a
big, mooshy chocolate cream pie, and there are probably moments when you literally ache to do exactly
that. But after treating yourself to that pie-in-the-face
daydream, get all the props together and crack into
making the desired impression. It can even be fun.

Cara is the brand-new vice-president and associate
merchandising director of a large Los Angeles sportswear company. Cara has read all the success books and
takes them seriously. The books say that the rules
about business dress do not apply to California, but
since Cara went there from the East, she follows them
rigidly and expects the women in her department to do
the same. Bunny, who had been there twelve years
when Cara got there, is a free-spirited slob who is determined not to wear a tailored suit and carry a brief-
case. She wears floor-length pioneer skirts with dust
ruffles, carries a dirty denim tote bag, and pretends not
to understand English when Cara holds forth at meetings about personal appearance and a "neat, crisp company look." Although she is a magnificent fashion de-

signer with a fine track record in "hot sales numbers,"
Bunny has just been fired. She clashed with Cara's vi-
sion of corporate style.

All across the United States, the trend toward acqui-
sitions and mergers is shaking up corporate structures
that were assumed to be unshakable. New executives
are making waves in peaceful company ponds, causing
consternation among "old guard" standbys who are resistant to change and determined to maintain the status
quo. In Atlanta a family-owned giant with a hundred-
year-old reputation for paternalism recently stirred,
rubbed its eyes, and made it known that the company
was coming into the twentieth century before the
twenty-first gets here. Most of the executives were one-
job people, including Joann who, at age fifty-five, had
been there twenty-four years and could retire at age
sixty with a bundle or at sixty-five with a bushel basket
full of money and other hard-earned retirement benefits.
Joann was a whiz at her job, with a national reputation
in her field. Under the new corporate structure, a new
"overview position" was created in her area and Joann
was invited to apply. She declined on grounds that she
was near retirement, had enough to do already, didn't
want to take on a lot of new responsibility at this stage
of the game, et cetera, et cetera, ad nauseum. A thirty-
five-year-old woman was recruited for the job, and
when she came in as Joann's boss, Joann had a smother-
ing spell. She was worse than uncooperative. She was
actively obstructive and encouraged everybody else to
be the same. "This company will never go along with
that New York swinger!" she assured them. Oh, but the
company did. The New York swinger tried to make a

friend of her, but when she could not, she simply moved Joann aside, gave her duties (*and* her large corner office) to a new executive recruit. Joann resigned in a huff.

First of all, Joann should have taken the "overview job." It *was* a promotion. But she had enjoyed Queen Bee status so long she didn't believe it could end, no matter what she did or did not do or who came along! Having declined the job, however, she should have welcomed the New York swinger, made a friend and ally of her, and demonstrated "indispensability" by supplying information and assistance only she could give. Since she overtly denied these, the new woman had to get the job done without Joann's cooperation, and once she found a way to do that, it was "Good-bye, Joann!" The fact that Joann was overweight and otherwise overcasual in her appearance didn't endear her to the sleek New Yorker either.

None of the political struggles in business is more anguishing than those between the "old guard" and the "new gang." The new gang feels obliged to make an immediate visible impact and is usually under mandate to do so. ("By God, this is costing plenty. Let's see some results!") The old guard feels equally obliged to keep things from getting out of hand. ("After all, we can't let people who don't know how things are around here upset the apple cart with a lot of crazy ideas that any fool can tell you won't work!")

Greta, who works for a Midwest food processor, was agonizing last summer over the interference of a new manager in her department, which she said he didn't "know beans" about. Greta had been there eight years and had developed a routine under which the department was functioning smoothly and effectively. She is a recognized authority in her field, having won several awards and been invited to speak on two occasions at the national convention of her industry.

"Now this new jerk comes in," Greta said, "and starts stirring up things with a lot of ideas that he thinks are red-hot and brand-new. They're not new to anybody but him and certainly not hot. He's pushing for things that I know won't work because we've already tried them—years ago—and I saw them fail with my own eyes. I've warned him but he keeps insisting. What can you do with a man that bullheaded?"

Someone else in her department explained it this way: the bullheadedness was largely response to Greta's attitude, which had been negative from the start. She was determined to keep running her department her way without any help from him and was, indeed, capable of doing exactly that. However, the new manager *was* the boss and this was made clear to her when he joined the firm. Her life would have been happier and she could have continued to do things pretty much her own way if she had greeted him with a friendly offer to review her department's activities for him, showing him what was going on and why. Naturally he feels he should make suggestions and she should give the man a chance. If his ideas have already been tried without success, she should point this out, tactfully, and go over the reasons with him, open-mindedly looking for ways that might make them work now. The fact that something failed in 1974 doesn't mean that it has to fail in 1980. Maybe it was an idea whose time hadn't come. At any rate, Greta can only appear bullheaded herself by refusing to consider his ideas even though they seem stupid to her. Worse still, she can seem "set in her ways," which is a euphemism for all kinds of unattractive conditions of body, mind, and spirit.

As for Greta's awards and speeches, she might have been taking those a little too seriously. "I think he's jealous of them!" she said. "He never won an industry award!" Neither did Greta—alone. She was backed by an excellent company whose policies permitted her to function at the top of her talent. She could never have gained any kind of industry recognition without the support of some astute people who have now brought in a "new gang." If they've made a mistake, they'll find it out. Meanwhile, Greta can only hurt herself. "I'm protecting my interests," she said. "By the time they find out they've made a mistake, it could be too late." Could be. But one thing is for sure: by being uncooperative and resistant, she can only make her problems worse. The manager is sure to complain that she's being bitchy, and not many women can ride out that one!

There have been whole books written on the subject of Sexual Politics and all that's left to say about *that* is: stay as far away from it as you can. The office romance used to be considered a fairly standard way for women to get ahead in business, and unquestionably there have been those who did. Women who lacked the ability (or the faith) to make it with their brains have elected to try it on their backs, and the success of a few with this ancient method is an embarrassment to many capable women today. The new business climate has changed the office-romance potential dramatically.

(A) Men look at women in the next office more as competitors than playmates—and vice versa.

(B) The broadcast and published reports on "Sexual Harassment" have frightened the company satyr.

(C) Both sexes are inclined to believe the risks aren't worth it.

Still, the problem does surface. At a Columbus, Ohio, meeting, a young woman said, "I know all about the dangers of getting fired if you're involved with men in the company, but what if the one who makes a pass at you is the top man—and you feel you've *got* to keep that job?"

Good question. I have heard of only one answer that men can accept without undergoing ego shock and that is, "There's somebody else."

Men have an incredible belief that they are paying a woman a compliment with a pass and suffer hurt pride and hurt feelings as well as anger when they are abruptly rebuffed.

"The hell with *his* pride and feelings and anger!" shouted a woman at the same meeting. "What about *mine*?" Another good question. The woman who had started the discussion did say he was the top man at the company and she felt that she had to keep the job. In that event, telling him that she has a previous commitment permits him to retreat unscathed by rejection.

At the same meeting another woman said, "I'm not involved but the man who owns our company is having an affair with a young woman who works there and they're so blatant that his wife is bound to find out. Everybody is talking about it."

Never mind what everybody is talking about. Keep your own mouth shut on the subject, even if you're dying to comment. It's none of your business.

Titillating as sex is as subject matter, it is not surprising that "sexual harassment" has become one of the "in" themes for the media and business seminars. Apparently men and women love to talk about it, although the fact is that most little girls, by the time they reach puberty, have become adept at handling a male come-on. If you are an executive or a woman on her way to becoming one, naïveté about sex or anything else is not going to speed you on your way. Whether the "passes" are directed at you or a young woman who works for you, you should be able to deal with the matter without starting World War III.

Sex-rooted horseplay around the office is always with us, and as long as both sexes are represented there, it isn't likely to disappear. Some of it is fun, most of it is high schoolish, and there are, of course, instances of it that are altogether reprehensible. You should be able to tell the difference and, when it gets out of hand, handle it smoothly.

If the pass is directed at you, tell the man pleasantly that your husband (or current love interest) is unreasonably, even murderously, jealous. "Let's pretend this didn't happen" is an innocuous statement that can get you both off the hook. (It's amazing how quickly it cools the romance when you let a man know his interest may be dangerous to himself.) If you are the boss and if it is directed at a young woman who reports to you, explain to her that no matter how crude it is, a pass indicates that the man is attracted to her—and explain to him, gently but firmly, that the office is not a dating bureau. If he continues to turn on the heat and it *is* a matter of genuine harassment, get him off the premises as fast as you can. The man has a deep problem and you shouldn't worry about anything he says about you as a result of your having fired him.

The golden touch in human relationships, that vaunted ability to "get along with people," is widely regarded as a mark of the most sought-after executive quality extant: leadership. Repeated indication that you don't hit it off with your associates can bog you down or bounce you out, no matter how good you are at your job. There *are* mavericks who make it in spite of their cantankerousness, but for every one of those, there must be thousands the world never heard of and never will. Being female compounds the problem.

Recently the personnel director of a large buying association that serves department stores told me he had "reluctantly decided" not to put a certain woman in charge of the company's West Coast operations, although she was extremely able, had been with the firm eleven years, and knew everything there was to know about the ins and outs of the job. "There's just one big drawback," he said. "Stella doesn't get along with people and that stopped me. She quarrels with everybody about the most unimportant things you ever heard of. Just saying good morning to her can start an argument. Some of the arguing, mind you, is good for the company—fights over the hard-nosed stuff like item changes and delivery dates. But a lot of it is so damned unnecessary. Little personality traits and very minor details concerned with how people go about doing things. It just makes everybody around her mad and tense and takes up a lot of time. We settled for a fellow who's not as knowledgeable—but everybody likes him."

Everybody likes him! The job may not be done as well but he keeps the troops happy. Stella should cut out the incidental carping and fault finding and bear down only on the important things directly concerning profit and loss to the company. Evidently she doesn't know the difference or doesn't bother to determine which is which. "We didn't hire her with instructions to try to change the human race," the personnel man said. "We just want her to help us run this business at a profit, and keeping the people around her happy enough to do their work well is a big part of it!"

Similarly, the head of a large executive placement firm phoned me about a woman of my acquaintance who had bombed twice on executive jobs he had recruited her for—both "choice spots with high starting salary, enormous perks, and top potential." He couldn't understand it. "She's nice as pie here. But at both places they had the same complaint. Said she gets everybody's back up. She's superqualified and they admit her work is damned near perfect but swear she can't get along with anybody—even her own secretary. At the last place they said she went through five secretaries in six weeks. Fought with everybody on the premises, *right up to the C.E.O.*—whose judgment she questioned in open meetings and on at least one memo circulated to the whole executive staff. She says they're all idiots! Bennington says her I.Q. is 153 and she's certainly a terrific talent—but the complaint I got at one place was that she's 'haughty and imperious' and at the other, that she's 'antagonistic.' What can be done with an attitude like that?"

Probably nothing—but I suggested he tell her you can't go around treating people like idiots even if you think they are. It's not "corporate leadership." I know the woman and know that she has very high standards, which she expects other people to measure up to regardless of whether they share her standards or her I.Q. But as long as she doesn't feel it part of her job to get along with people, she won't get along in the corporate structure.

The recruiter who was concerned about her two failures was concerned largely about his own reputation, since his income derives from retainers paid him by corporations. He will not recommend her now without mentioning her personality problem and says, "The minute I do that, they ask who else I have!"

Personal feuds pop up like weeds in all businesses, usually as a result of rivalry, but getting involved in one, no matter how justified you may feel, is childish. Since women and children are already closely associated in the male mind, consider yourself in double jeopardy.

Patricia had reason to dislike and resent a junior executive at her firm, a young man who habitually attacked her ideas and "automatically disagreed" with anything she said in meetings. They were both candidates for the job of a man who was retiring at the end of 1979, and Patricia's record was so outstanding, it was clear that she had the inside track. As the end of the year approached, Patricia's rival stepped up his attacks and tart criticisms until finally she was goaded into "blowing up" at a meeting—which was exactly what he wanted her to do. She told him off at the top of her voice in the presence of four other people (all men) and felt wonderful about it—until it was announced two weeks later that the young man was getting the promotion instead of Patricia.

"I protested, of course," she told me. "I should have had that job! All my credentials were better—performance, experience, education, everything! But I was told that I had to learn to control myself, that I mustn't be emotional in business situations and must get along with people even when we disagree."

Patricia has learned a lesson, but it was a costly one. She knows now that she should have made the young man's attacks on her work look as unreasonable as they really were by replying to them calmly, supporting her ideas with quietly stated facts. Everybody realized that he was goading her and, as long as she took it with equanimity, her associates were on her side. But when she finally exploded, it was an ugly scene that was embarrassing to them and they deserted her. "Female instability" was the way it came off to that room full of men.

A vital element in getting along with people is compromise, and nobody of my acquaintance understands this better than Julie Hoover—or has more reason to! Julie is the East Coast vice-president at ABC-TV, in charge of broadcast standards and practices. That means her office decides what can and what cannot go into the commercials and programs you see on television. It means that she must somehow make decisions that are acceptable to the advertisers, their advertising agencies, the F.T.C., F.C.C., and other government

agencies, the American Broadcasting Company's legal
department, programming department, and God alone
knows what other departments—to say nothing of the
viewing audience or the executive staffs at the ABC-
affiliated television stations in over two hundred cities
from New York to Los Angeles.

I can sympathize with Julie's problems, having once
spent three days trying to explain to a client why an
airline commercial can show a gorgeous girl undulating
out of the ocean in less than ten square inches of bikini,
though his commercial for a brassiere may not display
the product on a living model. (The ruling is based on
the fact that the airline commercial is not selling bikinis
but plane tickets to the Caribbean, while his commercial is selling brassieres. But try to convince a brassiere
retailer that this is a valid difference and let me hear
from you!)

At any rate, Julie is an authority on judicious compromise and she spoke feelingly on the subject at the
YWCA career session where she joined Barbara Smith
and me in the panel discussion of Positive Manipulation. Julie said, "There are very few absolutes in life—
very few situations that are all black or all white—and
this is particularly true in business. Executives frequently start from absolute positions at opposite poles
but they gradually make trade-offs that move them
from their start-up polar positions into middle ground.
Each side makes reasonable compromises until an
agreement is reached that everyone can live with. It's a
matter of give-and-take all the way, so that there are
rarely total blacks or total whites in business—only
varying shades of gray."

Julie says that she does not believe in generalities

about her sex any more than she believes in black-and-white situations. "But," she adds, "I suppose if I felt constrained to make a general statement on the subject, I'd have to say that in my experience, women are more likely to take an all-black or all-white stance than men. This, in my opinion, shouldn't be. Only the grays are operative."

That's the color of politics: gray. And maybe you don't like gray a bit. But whether you feel exhilarated by the excitement of office politics or find the whole matter sick-making, give yourself these breaks:

1. *Get the job done.* Don't stop to worry about whether you're being manipulative or Managing by Motivation. Business is Results oriented. (The capital R belongs to the territory.)

2. *Get along with everybody.* Getting along with your peers makes the job easier as well as more pleasant. And unless you get along with your boss, the rest doesn't matter.

3. *If you're the old guard, give the new gang enough rope.* If they're good, they'll skip it and you'll skip along with them; if they're not, you'll be there for the hanging.

4. *If you're the new gang, remember that the people who've been around awhile know a lot that can be useful.* Even though you don't plan to use any of it, listen respectfully. You may hear something that will make you change your mind.

5. *No matter which group you belong to, don't forget that your paycheck comes from the company.* Office feuds are never good for business.

6. *Don't assume that an idea that failed ten years ago won't succeed brilliantly with a new twist.* Then was then, now is now. The fact that it laid an ostrich egg then doesn't mean it won't produce a peacock this time around. If it's what your new boss suggests, kid glove it!

7. *Don't be lulled into an assumption that "workaholism" is in widespread disrepute.* Most great businesses were started and built by workaholics and are kept going by them. Even on the golf course, on skis, in his favorite saloons, and with his favorite people, the boss still has business on the brain and cherishes every little symptom of workaholism in his employees. Recently I heard it summed up by a C.E.O. who was irritated by the shortcomings of an executive on his staff. "I know he does stupid things," he said, "but I'll say this much for him: he's not lazy. The sonofabitch *does* work!"

Recipes for Success

Chapter 11

"Everybody is looking for a guarantee!"

So am I. So are you. So are the men and women you work for and the ones who work for you. Aware though we all are that there's no such thing as a sure thing, the search for one never stops. And while the search goes on, so does the gamble. American business puts billions on the line every day. As an individual, you bet your life.

"But I only want my job to be a living—not my life!" I hear this all around the country, but not as much today as several years back, when job levels that now are open to women were closed to them. This is, of course, an entirely worthy wish that takes us back to square one and what it is that you really want. The fact is that if you want advancement, career fulfillment, or whatever it seems more respectable to call it, your job is an

enormously important part of your life, measurable
only in terms of your ambition.

Every time we make a deal, there is the hope
(spoken or not) that *this* one will do it. This one will
make us rich or richer, happy or happier, free, somehow, or freer. Even if the deal is minor, there is a glim-
mer of expectation that it is a magic move toward pie in
the sky, and while a lot depends on what other people
do, how it comes out on your side depends mainly on
you. Work is the key.

"Unless you put in more hours, dedication, and con-
centration, you will not make it," says George Ball,
president of E. F. Hutton, the brokerage firm. His company's advertising slogan is "When E. F. Hutton talks,
people listen," and about 130 pairs of ears were standing
at attention when he spoke at a two-day conference on
women in the work force at New York's Sheraton-St.
Regis Hotel early in 1980. The conference was spon-
sored jointly by the *Ladies' Home Journal* and the
American Telephone & Telegraph Company. (A.T.&T.,
it will be remembered, was one of the first companies in
the United States to offer employment to women, and
while, for years, "the girls" there didn't have much to
say about anything beyond "Number, Please?" women
did get their first career break at the telephone company.)

According to *The New York Times*, George Ball told
the conference, "There is no room for balance if you
want to get to the top in business." *Times* reporter Enid
Nemy said he described competition for jobs at the top
as "terrible" and observed that people attracted to them
might be described as eccentric. He said that they are

required and willing to make sacrifices—among the sacrifices, accommodating their lives to a work week often averaging seventy and eighty hours.

Stephen I. D'Agostino, the food industry's young rocket, disagrees only numerically. "I'd say seventy to eighty hours a week is a low estimate," he said in a telephone interview. Steve is head of Manhattan's D'Agostino supermarket chain and vice-chairman of the National Food Marketing Institute, but emphasized that he was speaking for himself, expressing a personal point of view. "It's more like twenty-four hours a day, seven days a week," he said. "Total commitment. Whatever you're doing, even 'relaxing,' you are relating everything that is going on to the commitment you've made, which never eases up or lets down. But that's true if you're at the top of anything. True of a musician, a painter—even a house painter. Or a housewife! Success at whatever you do takes all you've got, all the time."

If there is, indeed, always room at the top, this may be the reason why—and why so few women aspire to occupy it. Needless to say, few women are both willing and equipped by circumstances to make a job commitment of that magnitude. The trade-offs include a sizable chunk of family life—and in some cases may include marriage and children altogether. A famous woman executive recently told me, "I couldn't do what I do if there was another living thing at home besides me. I couldn't take care of a dog or a cat or a bird or even a goldfish. It's all I can do to stay on top of my job and look after myself." I know what she means!

Is it worth it?

Last November I was asked that question in Denver by a delightful young television interviewer, Linda Scott, at station KOA-TV. My reply was, "It depends on what day you ask me." And it does! Some days the answer is a reverberating "No!" but I'm sure the negative is shared from time to time by my friends who are musicians, housewives, house painters, poets, and bookies.

Only you can determine the size of your commitment, where it should be put to work, and how. Women, not only unaccustomed to job decisions but until recently resigned to the idea that they might never get a chance to make them, have devoured books, articles, and seminar programs on success, power, progress, and simple survival in business.

Patty O'Toole, a business writer who has read most of these books and covered *beaucoup* conferences and seminars, says, "The sad fact is that most women who attend these business seminars have nothing to do with the hard-nosed, bottom-line decisions that govern hiring, firing, raises, and promotions. The most notorious [misdirections] come from the dress-for-success, self-packaging school but perhaps the most damaging are the retreaded ideas from the human potential movement —psychologists selling management sensitivity and better communication." Writing in *Redbook* magazine about seminar rip-offs, O'Toole adds: "Unfortunately, these concepts do not translate well from couch to corporation because they emphasize the worker rather than the work."

Since I am an author of some of the books and articles, and have been a speaker at no fewer than two dozen of the seminars, I earnestly hope they have been

helpful. They can suggest. They can give you some in-
sights from the experience of other people. They can let
you know you are not alone. But I cannot overempha-
size the conviction I have that there is no such thing
as a "success recipe."

I will never forget visiting the office of an attorney
who kept clasping his hands behind his head, leaning as
far back in his chair as the swivel would go, and staring
at the ceiling. Finally, I was unable to quell my curi-
osity about the ceiling's attraction and, reluctantly,
looked up there, too. I saw a small strip of paper taped
to the acoustical tile but was unable to read what was
written on it.

"I'm sorry," I said. "I can't stand it. I have to know
what's written on the paper."

"Oh, *that!*" he laughed. "Just something I put up
there a long time ago as a reminder. It just says: THE
ANSWER IS NOT UP HERE!"

The answer is not on the ceiling, not at a seminar, not
in any article or book. Thomas Edison said, "There are
no lengths to which a man will not go to avoid thinking," and if Edison's time was now, his homily would
certainly be revised to include women. The answer is in
our own heads. After we've worked it out there, we
proceed by invoking our guts.

The new freedoms serve in some ways to dramatize
the old familiar restrictions and restraints. Women
often feel in a "no win" situation, excluded from the old
boys' network, excluded from the informal business dis-
cussions that take place on the golf course, on hunting
and fishing trips, and numerous other occasions that are
strictly stag.

Toni, a friend of mine in Cincinnati, told me how put-down she felt when she applied for a promotion. Her company was a manufacturer of "light" industrial products and she was qualified by education, on-the-job training, and experience to move into a higher executive spot that had opened up. "No way!" the personnel director told her. "In that kind of job, some of the most important decisions that are made are made in the men's room."

Toni said she was so stunned by the reply that she left immediately. "I was so confused, I didn't know what else to do."

The reply was a classic cop-out and had the desired effect. It got Toni out of the office of a man who has concretized ideas about job gender and doesn't want women adding to his toils by applying for that kind of position. By making her feel that her application was tantamount to a demand that she be allowed to use the men's plumbing facilities, he threw her into confused flight. His riposte probably made him chuckle all day with self-satisfaction. Of course, the men's room is no place to make a business decision or any other kind of decision, except whether to see a doctor, but you can't tell that to an old-fashioned personnel director. Don't try.

Toni's best bet was to play it very cool, smile, remain pleasant and nonargumentative—if she wanted to keep the job she had. Men have been saying things like that for so long that some of them still believe it. When they really do, there's no effective way to deal with it, since making them feel as ridiculous as they are can cost you not only the job you want but the job you've got.

After two agonizing days Toni solved her problem by

speaking privately with the man she would report to in
the new job. His thinking was more enlightened than
the personnel director's and he was pleased to know of
her interest in the job. After reviewing her credentials,
he requested that she be transferred to the position.
"I'm sure the personnel director knew what had happened," Toni said, "but he didn't say anything. Just
looked the other way when we met. He's never forgiven
me but he retires next year anyway."

It should be noted that this is an extremely dangerous tactic that wouldn't work at all in a large corporation. The bigger the companies are, the more rigid are
the rules about channels, and employees are expected to
stay in them. Toni's ploy, however, was the "end run"
that men use to advantage all the time. It is not unusual
for a department manager or a division head to request
a specific person for an opening—but if he or she doesn't
want you and you've made an end run in that direction,
you could be in trouble. The idea is to be the kind of
executive material these key people need for their own
advancement—and get them asking for you. How do
you do that? Let them know you'd like to work for
them. It's always flattering—and indicates to everyone
else around that they're going places. Just don't step on
the blue suede shoes of your present superior in the
process. Nobody should hate you for wanting to do as
well as you can—but it happens.

I wish I had all the answers on my ceiling but I don't.
Only you can find yours, because every work situation
is exquisitely and devastatingly different, involving
people who are fundamentally the same wherever you
go but exquisitely and devastatingly different in such

telling details as what frightens, excites, or delights them.

Business is constantly compared to games—traditionally ball games and more lately the "think games," notably chess. Although the terminology belonged to the forties and fifties, we still hear people talk about the Newspaper Game, the Real Estate Game, the Insurance Game—possibly a hangover from the Broadway show and subsequent film called *The Pajama Game*.

Worn though the terminology is, the comparison remains valid because every move you make brings about a responding move, a whole series of moves, a chain reaction. ("Did *I* do that!") ("You *did* it, sweetie!") If that sounds frightening, it's only because it is.

Are there real cracks in the wall of resistance to female executives? Some observers think so. Even male observers. One of these, Dolf Zapfel, columnist for *Home Furnishings Daily*, looks at the housewares industry and is cheered by the sight of three female executives among heaven knows how many men. Confessing thirty years of puzzlement over the absence of women in the upper areas of an industry whose wares are so closely allied to activities that are traditionally female, Zapfel cites the successes of Ingrid Berg, president of Ingrid, Inc., the $25-million-a-year company she founded with her husband in Chicago; Sue Marchand, the able president of Irwinware, founded by her father and uncle in New York; and Gwen Kestel, director of marketing for Burwood Products in Chicago.

Zapfel quotes Kestel as believing that "male chauvinism is no longer chic" and that there is a definite awareness evolving among men in business about women and that they can no longer be ignored. (One hopes!) According to Zapfel, she "feels, however, that women still have to come into the business world with higher standards and more elaborate backgrounds," and resents the fact that hard-hitting men are considered "aggressive" and are applauded for it while ambitious women are labeled "pushy." (No comment.)

In June, 1979, Lenore Hershey, editor in chief of *Ladies' Home Journal,* asked several dozen businesswomen to "draft a short personal statement about women in the next decade." Realizing that Jeane Dixon has nothing to fear from me, I sent Lenore the following:

"Anyone who attempts to predict the future is out on a shaky limb with the weatherman. What happens to women in the eighties will depend largely on what happens in the world (period), since such exigencies as war, economic collapse, and natural or man-made disasters could, of course, change everything.

"Barring these extremities, women will, in all likelihood, hang onto their gains of the sixties and seventies. This will be particularly true in the business world, where there is an ever-growing need for real capability, and where there are never enough 'good' people to go around. Businesses, caught in the economic squeeze, can no longer afford to tolerate substandard performance from men who simply 'can't hack it' when there are women available right on the premises who can do the job brilliantly—and are burning to prove it.

"In the eighties women will fare better in the executive suite because they are realizing the importance of corporate politics and learning to 'play the game.' This does not mean that they can get away with shoddy performance, but that they must learn to match capability with finesse.

"A lot of women in the seventies have been toppled from lofty executive positions, not because they couldn't do the job, but because they underestimated or misunderstood the political situation in the company. In the eighties they will be more politically astute because they will have had more opportunity to observe, experience, and learn in the sensitive upper echelons of business—where, until recently, they were only rarely admitted."

Geraldine Rhoads, the distinguished editor of *Woman's Day*, the magazine with a female readership of over seventeen million, says this:

"I've worked with at least a hundred [genuine career women] and for the one who is devious, there are ten who level with you.

"The women bosses have been secure in their authority (all but one), and fair and helpful. My first was a mentor whose philosophy stayed with me long after I moved on to other bosses. She herself had been inspired by one of the founding feminists, M. Carey Thomas. She said that 'a woman can do anything she really sets out to do,' and although I knew that the catch was in the word 'really,' I believed her.

"Right now, there's a lot more cause to think that way, though I worry about some of our newcomers. They're ever so capable, and I'm happy that in this more or less enlightened age, they start out early knowing what they want to be and do, but they expect the 'career path' to be a lot straighter and easier than such roads almost ever are, and some of them just won't make it, on that account, and won't ever know why. They don't know how much they must *really* put up with to move to the top. I think affirmative action and the women's movement, both great boons to us for sure, have conned some of them into thinking that advancement is automatic.

"Most feminine traits serve women well in their careers, although I know more businesswomen than men who want everyone to like them, and who feel a need to like everyone with whom they work. Impossible! Of course. Some of the people you like the least are important to you as colleagues, and the more you succeed, the less you can count on being universally loved.

"By this I don't mean that women are petty and given to tantrums or crybaby reactions or bickering or prima donna tactics. That they 'don't get along.' In fact, if I think hard about all the people with whom I've worked, I believe I've known more men who stooped to such ploys, and I grow angry that they then attribute these tendencies to women.

"Most career women are stable as well as smart and productive and supportive and adventurous and genuinely ambitious. In saying so, I'm able to compare them favorably with men of real talent and drive and stability; I've been lucky in many of my male bosses and associates, too."

If my life were scheduled for a rerun, I would unhesitatingly go into business again. I don't know whether my chances today would be better or worse than they were thirty years ago when there were fewer committed

career women around, but I do know that competition
heats up only when opportunity rises and the presence
of one means that the other is there in abundance. At
any rate, here are some of the things I would tell myself:

1. *Don't waste time looking for a guarantee,* and
if anybody offers you one, examine both sides of it
carefully—preferably with an attorney. Job guarantees are loosely as reliable as bills of sale for the
Brooklyn Bridge, and although the intentions of
your guarantor may be pure as Ivory soap, time
does change everything.

2. *Listen very attentively to what is being promised you* and try to hear what is actually being
said. All of us tend to hear what we want to hear
and revise the words or fill in the blanks to fit our
hopes.

A woman I'll call Denny McPherson went to
New Orleans as the Louisiana sales manager for
an excellent line of household products. The man
who hired her told Denny that her salary plus
commissions should easily bring her an income of
$60,000 a year. She was so enchanted with the idea
of earning so much money that she didn't hear the
word "should" and was shattered when she ended
up earning less than $20,000. Even so, she fared
better than the woman I'll call Reba Gilly, who
was guaranteed a six-figure salary in two years.
Lured by promise of a six-figure income and part
ownership, she left a $40,000-a-year job to join a
company that went into bankruptcy seven months

later. Denny should have been listening instead of counting her money, and Reba should not have made a move without a thorough investigation of the company. Women make commitments for themselves on slender evidence that they wouldn't dream of accepting in a decision they were making for their companies.

3. *Self-interest is not necessarily selfish.* When you do the best you can for yourself, it's usually best for your job and your gender, too. If charity begins at home, altruism begins in your own shoes. You can't possibly help anybody else until you've acquired the requisite strength—which means, first of all, looking after yourself.

4. *Enjoy your job and if you don't, quit,* no matter how much you're being paid. Life's too short to seem so long and it seems interminable when you've got a job you hate. Even if you work only a few hours a week, it should be at something you feel good about, something that is a growing experience and a happy one, too. Susan Hotz, president of the Denver Advertising Federation, summed it up wonderfully last November when she said, "The Saturday morning when I wake up thinking Thank God I don't have to go to work for two whole days, or the Monday morning when I get dressed for the office thinking Lord how can You do this to me for another whole week?—that's when I'll know it's time to shove off and get myself another job. To me the work I'm doing now is like being in love. And I'm a newlywed!"

5. *If you do quit, quit on your own timetable.*

Think it through, make a plan, and be ready to continue without income interruption unless you have enough funds available to keep you going while you're making your move.

6. *There is always choice.* (Repeat, *always.*) Maybe you think there are no alternatives, but that's only because you haven't thought your situation and yourself all the way through. In his extraordinary book called *The Best Way in the World for a Woman to Make Money*, David King explores the opportunities in selling—an option that is open in one way or another to absolutely anybody who can work at all. You don't like to sell? Everything involves selling, because anything that gets done, made, performed, produced, sung, recited, or played has to be sold at some point. No matter what else you call it, you're selling all day.

Last year, I was on a seminar program with a young woman who made a sensational presentation, tracing her firm's development of a shopping mall. She is a graduate architect, duly pleased at her standing in a "man's field." She was followed on the program by David King, who did his usual inspirational job—which inspired her to scrawl a note across my pad: "Isn't he wonderful? Makes me wish I could sell but I despise it." I looked at her closely and realized that she couldn't be more serious—although she had just done one of the finest selling jobs I'd ever witnessed!

7. *Respect the work that supports your life-style.* Maybe you hate it, maybe you feel stuck with it, maybe you feel it's beneath you—and maybe it is.

But if you take money for it, do it as well as you can. Having spent my life in the advertising business, I have worked with art directors, copywriters, and commercial film producers who are frustrated Picassos, Nevelsons, Faulkners, Flannery O'Connors, Fellinis, and Lina Wertmullers. The admirable ones were those who made peace with their choices and gave them everything they had to offer—realizing that you never get a chance to do better things unless you do the lesser ones really well.

8. *Accept the quirks and idiosyncrasies of your associates*, and don't break your heart or spoil your own chances trying to change them. You've got your share of these nitty little traits that drive people up the wall and your own are the only ones you have a real chance to do something about.

Carol Moberg, founder of the Manhattan public relations firm that operates under her name, cannily observes: "You can't really change job habits of adult professionals. It's easier to live with them than put yourself through the wringer trying to get people to do things your way. Who knows? Maybe theirs is better. Anyway, it must be for them!"

9. *Be willing to take the same kind of risk you expect other people to take.* A job is a covenant and when you take one or give one, it's a mutual bet, with a chance for profit or loss on both sides. No matter which side you're on, if it doesn't go your way, don't whine about it. Correct the mistake as quickly as you can and with as little damage to yourself as possible.

10. *Identify with Management.* If you expect to be a part of it yourself, it's the only way to go. That doesn't mean turning your back on the problems of nonmanagement people. Quite the contrary. Management has a continuing responsibility to the people who work in every area of the company, and the ability to see *their* point of view is a valued executive trait.

11. *Be enthusiastic.* Business does ride on confidence and optimism, and the more you have, the happier you'll be whether it takes you further or not.

12. *Mark yourself up.* Always look and sound as though you belong on the next step up. That requires working, thinking, and, in all probability, trying harder. Bitching about it can be fun, but getting what you want is more so. Go for it!

Index